D1578282

D. MONK

PITMAN'S SHORTHAND

NEW COURSE

NEW ERA EDITION

Isaac Pitman

LONDON
SIR ISAAC PITMAN & SONS, LTD.

COPYRIGHT

This edition of Sir Isaac Pitman's system of Shorthand is the exclusive copyright of Sir Isaac Pitman & Sons, Ltd., and it will be an infringement of such copyright if matter from it be reproduced in any publication without written permission.

ALL RIGHTS RESERVED

SIR ISAAC PITMAN & SONS, Ltd.
PITMAN HOUSE, PARKER STREET, KINGSWAY, LONDON, W.C.2
THE PITMAN PRESS, BATH
PITMAN HOUSE, BOUVERIE STREET, CARLTON, MELBOURNE
22–25 BECKETT'S BUILDINGS, PRESIDENT STREET, JOHANNESBURG

ASSOCIATED COMPANIES

PITMAN MEDICAL PUBLISHING COMPANY, Ltd.
39 PARKER STREET, LONDON, W.C.2

PITMAN PUBLISHING CORPORATION
2 WEST 45TH STREET, NEW YORK

SIR ISAAC PITMAN & SONS (CANADA), Ltd.
(INCORPORATING THE COMMERCIAL TEXT BOOK COMPANY)
PITMAN HOUSE, 381–383 CHURCH STREET, TORONTO

PRINTED BY HAZELL WATSON & VINEY LTD
LEIGH ROAD, SLOUGH AND AYLESBURY

PREFACE

ISAAC PITMAN published the first edition of his shorthand system in 1837. He spent half a century improving it, and the great work has since been continued by several generations of expert writers and teachers.

Millions have used this system as a means of earning a livelihood, and today, throughout the world, wherever accurate and immediately legible recording of spoken English is required, in Parliaments and Congresses, in the Courts of Justice, and in offices of every size and sort, there is Pitman's Shorthand, doing what no machine can do, reproducing speech, the whole speech and nothing but the speech (with whatever helpful notes the intelligent recorder may choose to append to the speech), in a form that can be read like a book as soon as it is written or ten years afterwards. No system has been tested for so long or by so many writers of such a wide diversity of natural aptitude; and no system has won so high a reputation in the crucible of experience.

DISTINCTIVE FEATURES OF THE SYSTEM

Isaac Pitman devised his system after a profound and epoch-making study of the phonetic structure of the English language. The system is a result of his scientific analysis. Systems before Pitman, and even some systems in use today, could achieve speed only through the laborious memorization of hundreds of special forms and arbitrary abbreviations. In Pitman's Shorthand, speed and facility of writing and safety of reading are achieved by following a coherent and comprehensive scheme: each individual sound has its sign, and sounds of the same family have signs with an appropriate family likeness, so that, after a little practice, the signs seem to produce themselves like snapshots from the sounds, and the sounds themselves seem to speak from the written page.

Handwriting Motion Inadequate. The consonants of the language are represented by a series of simple strokes, selected to provide the most facile joinings with one another. Because these strokes do not follow the slope of ordinary longhand writing, they can be formed with complete distinctiveness when they are joined together and written with great speed. The purpose of shorthand is to represent letters as briefly and as distinctively as possible. *The adoption of a uniform slope in a shorthand system would result in a confusing similarity* *of consonants*, and the hand of the writer would be retarded because of the necessity for careful and laborious representation of fine distinctions.

Pairing of Consonants. In certain cases consonants are paired because of their similarity of sound. The first consonant in the pair is pronounced lightly (as "S") and is unvoiced, and the second consonant in the pair is the corresponding heavy sound (as "Z") and is voiced. The same stroke is used for both consonants, but for the first consonant a light stroke is written, and the second stroke of the pair is written with a slight pressure of the pen. *This avoids the necessity of employing different strokes to represent similarly sounded consonants.* If, for instance, half- and double-length strokes were used to represent these pairs, valuable shorthand abbreviating material would be lost, which in Pitman's Shorthand is used to represent the addition of letters and even whole syllables. *The use of this device thus saves time and labour for the shorthand writer and involves no extra penmanship.*

Elimination of Vowel Signs. Words are represented by a complete shorthand outline of their consonants. Short forms, or "word signs," are few in number. Circles, loops and hooks are used for the representation of frequently occurring and natural combinations of consonants in English words. In the application of this abbreviating material the presence or absence of a vowel is indicated, and it is unnecessary to write signs for the vowel sounds. *Here again the shorthand writer is saved much time and labour.* A series of disjoined vowel signs is provided for insertion where necessary, such as in isolated words, or proper names.

Position Writing. Position writing is a simple and effective device for the indication of vowels. Writing a word above, on, or through the line, according to its first vowel sound, *is another means of expressing sound without actual writing, and it is a device highly prized by the fastest writers.* Generations of the best writers in the world have proved that the most effective means of securing compact, swift and legible shorthand outlines is through complete representation of the consonants, and that the insertion of the vowel signs is a needless waste of the writer's labour.

Summary. In Pitman's Shorthand the amount of actual writing has been reduced to a minimum because of the scientific use of the stenographic abbreviating material. Circles, loops, hooks, halving and doubling are devices used for the representation of syllables, and not for the formation of an alphabet. An adequate skill in shorthand writing is developed through the application of the abbreviating principles of the system. These devices are few in number, and they are easily understood and applied. Writers do not have to resort to such doubtful expedients as memorizing large numbers of specially contracted forms or writing only the first part of words, in order to keep pace with a speaker. They are able to develop their skill in accurate note taking without arbitrary memorization and with a minimum of labour. The simple principles of the system permit its writers to maintain and increase their skill, to their own satisfaction and to the satisfaction of those whose utterances they undertake to record.

FEATURES OF THE BOOK

This book presents the principles of Pitman's Shorthand in a logical arrangement. The principles are stated briefly and simply, and each statement is followed by an adequate amount of application. The work of the teacher is made easier by dividing the principles into small units of construction.

An unusual feature of the book is the wealth of drill material provided for each unit of instruction. The amount of this material is more than that appearing in any shorthand textbook previously issued. The exercises have been so compiled that they are similar in subject matter to the material dictated to students in later stages of the study of the subject. The development of skill in reading and writing these exercises is therefore of great importance, for they provide practice as valuable to the student as the dictation he will receive when the principles have been completed. Realization of this will encourage the student and will stimulate rapid progress. The exercises provide a cumulative review of the principles and of the short forms.

In the application of the principles a vocabulary of the two thousand commonest words has been used. Less frequently occurring words are used occasionally, however, to provide additional illustrations and to demonstrate in the exercises the application of a principle to similar words. These additional words are always well within the average student's vocabulary.

Most of the exercises are in shorthand. Reading correct shorthand is invaluable to the student, and the reading approach makes it possible to prevent students from writing or seeing incorrectly written outlines, and in this way assists them to write accurately from the start. The shorthand exercises are also useful for home preparation and from Chapter IX onwards longhand exercise or dictation material is included.

Dictation is always interesting to the student, and teachers will find *Graded Dictation Studies* of great use to them when used side by side with the NEW COURSE. In this book there is a wealth of dictation material arranged so as to correspond accurately with the chapters of the NEW COURSE and at the same time progressively graded by word-frequency. Complete practice for dictation purposes is also given in the whole vocabulary of each chapter of the NEW COURSE, including short forms, phrases and word lists.

The very frequently used words expressed in shorthand by some logical principle of abbreviation are introduced in their appropriate places in the text and are also given in three alphabetically arranged lists at the end of the volume. The first list gives those short forms that are included in the text and these all come within the two thousand commonest words. The second list gives additional short forms occurring in the first ten thousand commonest words, and the third list a few others which do not occur in the ten thousand commonest words. It will be noticed that for all ordinary purposes the first list is adequate and in fact represents between 50 and 60 per cent of average matter.

When the book has been completed *A Student's Review of Pitman's Shorthand* will be found most useful for a re-learning of the principles by a quite different approach and also provides abundant material for reading and dictation. The *Second Session Dictation Course, Elementary Examination Speed Tests* and *Business Letters for Dictation* will be found of value for the further development of skill in writing shorthand for business purposes. Literature available for reading in shorthand is listed in the *Pitman Shorthand and Typewriting Catalogue. Pitman's Office Training* published weekly includes many shorthand pages and regular articles for the guidance of the shorthand writer, and further shorthand reading material will be found in the monthly issues of *Pitman's Business Education.*

CONTENTS

INTRODUCTION

SHORTHAND is the art of representing spoken sounds by written signs. Pitman's Shorthand provides a way of representing every sound heard in English words.

Ordinary longhand spelling is seldom phonetic. Pitman's Shorthand is phonetic; that is, words are generally written as they are sounded and not according to ordinary longhand spelling. With certain exceptions no signs are used that are not wanted to represent the sound.

The following illustrations show how to think of the words when writing shorthand—

palm	is *p-ah-m*	*wrought*	is *r-aw-t*
pale	is *p-ay-l*	*coal*	is *k-oh-l*
key	is *k-ee*	*tomb*	is *t-oo-m*

With the exception of *worsted* (the woollen material) and a few proper names, e.g. *Worcester*, if an R appears in the spelling of a word it always appears in the shorthand. Words that include a "silent R" in some pronunciations of English are thus made much easier to read, e.g. *iron, park*.

The shorthand characters should be made as neatly and as accurately as possible. The size of the shorthand strokes in this book is a good standard to adopt in your own writing. The signs join readily with one another and they can be written with great speed when practised sufficiently. Resist the temptation to sacrifice accurate formation for speed. Speed in writing will naturally follow the practice of neat and accurate writing.

CHAPTER I

1. The First Six Consonants

The sounds heard in English words are, in Pitman's Shorthand, divided into—

Twenty-four Consonants　　Twelve Vowels　　Four Diphthongs

A shorthand sign is provided for each of these sounds.

The first six consonants are represented by straight strokes written downward—

Letter	Sign	Name	As in
P		pee	pay, ape, up
B		bee	bay, Abe, be
T		tee	Tay, ate, it
D		dee	day, aid, do
CH		chay	chest, etch, which
J		jay	jest, edge, age

The arrows indicate the direction in which the strokes are written. They are never written in any other direction.

NOTE: These consonants form pairs: *p* and *b*, *t* and *d*, *ch* and *j*. In each pair a *light* sound is represented by a *light* stroke, and a corresponding *heavy* sound is represented by a *heavier* stroke.

2. Vowel ā

Vowels are represented by dots and dashes written alongside the consonant strokes. When a vowel comes *before* a consonant, it is placed *before* the stroke (left side); when a vowel comes *after* a consonant, it is placed *after* the stroke (right side).

1

The long vowel *ā* is represented by a heavy dot—

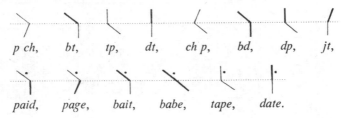

ape,   pay,   Abe,   bay,   eight,   aid,   day,   age.

Write the consonant stroke first, and then place the vowel sign. Two light dashes underneath an outline indicate that the word represented begins with a capital letter.

NOTE: There are three places alongside a stroke in which vowels may be written—beginning, middle, and end, or first, second, and third place. The dot for long *ā* is written in the middle place, and it is therefore called a "second-place vowel."

3. Joining of Consonants

Consonants are joined without lifting the pen, as in longhand. Begin the second where the first ends, and write the stroke in its proper direction. Note that the first stroke rests on the line.

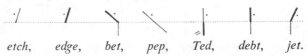

p ch,   bt,   tp,   dt,   ch p,   bd,   dp,   jt,

paid,   page,   bait,   babe,   tape,   date.

4. Vowel ĕ

Short *ĕ* is represented by a light dot, and is a second-place vowel—

etch,   edge,   bet,   pep,   Ted,   debt,   jet.

NOTE: The first stroke rests on the line. Write the consonant outline first, and then place the vowel sign.

5. Short Forms for Common Words

A few very frequently used words, such as *be, it, the, to,* are expressed in shorthand by a single sign. These short forms promote speedy writing, and they should be thoroughly memorized—

be,   it,   do,   which,   the,   to,   two or too,

but,   who.

6. Phrasing

As an aid to rapid writing, shorthand words may often be joined. This is called phrasing. Outlines should be phrased only when they join easily and naturally, as shown in the examples throughout this textbook. The first word in a phrase is written in its normal position—

to do,   *but which.*

A small tick *at the end* of a word represents *the*. The tick is written either upward or downward, whichever forms the sharper angle but, whether written upward or downward, its angle to the line of writing is always the same—

to the,   be the,   do the,   which the,   pay the,   paid the.

7. Punctuation

The following special punctuation marks are used in shorthand—

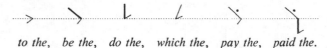

full stop,   question,   exclamation,   hyphen,   dash,   parenthesis.

Other signs are written as in longhand.

Exercise 1

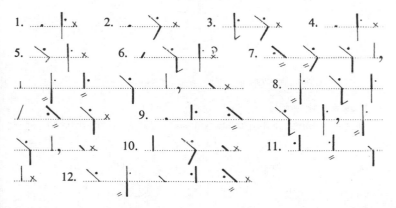

CHAPTER II

8. The Second Group of Consonants

The next four pairs of consonants are curves, and they are written downward—

Letter	Sign	Name	As in	Short Form for
F	⤜	ef	few, safe, for	
V	⤜	vee	view, save, have	*have* ⟍
TH	⟍(	ith	*th*igh, ba*th*, *th*ink	*think* (
TH	⟍(	thee	*th*y, ba*th*e, *th*em	*them* (
S	⟍)	ess	seal, ice, us	
Z	⟍)	zee	zeal, eyes, was	*was*)
SH	⟍	ish	she, wish, shall	*shall* ⟋
ZH	⟍	zhee	measure, treasure, usual	*usual/ly* ⟋

(a) *they,   say,   fade,   faith,   shape,   bathe,   shade.*

(b) *fed,   fetch,   death,   shed,   essay.*

9. Vowels ō and ŭ

Long *ō* is represented by a heavy dash, and is a second-place vowel—

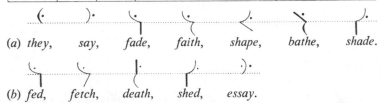

toe,   oat,   bow,   Joe,   foe,   oath,   so,   owes,

show,   showed,   boat,   both,   vote.

4

Short *ŭ* is represented by a light dash, and is a second-place vowel—

up,   us,   tub,   touch,   Dutch,   judge.

Exercise 2

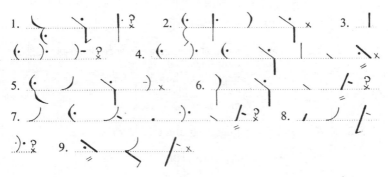

Exercise 3

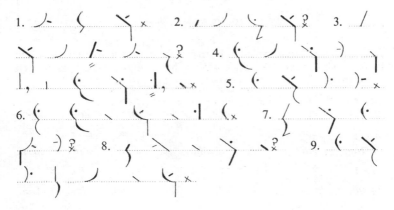

CHAPTER III

10. The Next Eight Consonants

The next eight consonants are all written forward. They are all light strokes except *g* and *ng*—

Letter	Sign	Name	As in	Short Form for
K		kay	cane, leak, come	*come*
G		gay	gain, league, give	*give* or *given*
M		em	may, seem, him	*him*
N		en	nay, seen, no	
NG		ing	long, sing, thing	*thing*
L		el	lay, coal, will	*lord*
W		way	weigh, aware, we	*we*
Y		yay	youth, yellow, yes	

When a vowel comes *before* a horizontal stroke it is written *above* the stroke; when a vowel comes *after* a horizontal stroke it is written *below* the stroke.

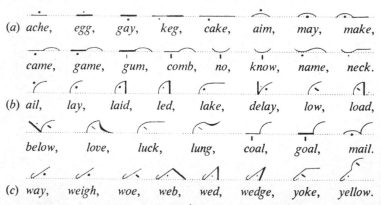

(a) ache, egg, gay, keg, cake, aim, may, make, came, game, gum, comb, no, know, name, neck.

(b) ail, lay, laid, led, lake, delay, low, load, below, love, luck, lung, coal, goal, mail.

(c) way, weigh, woe, web, wed, wedge, yoke, yellow.

6

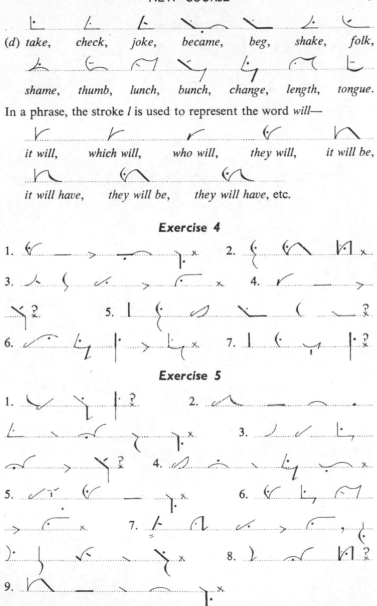

(d) take, check, joke, became, beg, shake, folk,

shame, thumb, lunch, bunch, change, length, tongue.

In a phrase, the stroke *l* is used to represent the word *will*—

it will, which will, who will, they will, it will be,

it will have, they will be, they will have, etc.

Exercise 4

1. 2.

3. 4.

5. 6. 7.

Exercise 5

1. 2.

 3.

 4.

5. 6.

 7.

 8.

9.

Exercise 6

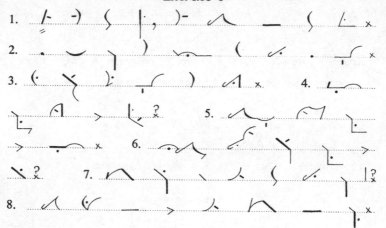

CHAPTER IV

11. First-place Vowels

The next four vowels are written in the *first* place, that is, at the beginning of a stroke. When the *first* vowel in a word is a *first-place* vowel, the outline is written in *first* position, that is, the first downstroke or upstroke in the outline is written *above* the line. First-position outlines consisting of horizontal strokes are written above the line.

(*a*) Long *ah* is represented by a heavy dot—

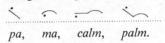

pa,   ma,   calm,   palm.

(*b*) Short *ă* is represented by a light dot—

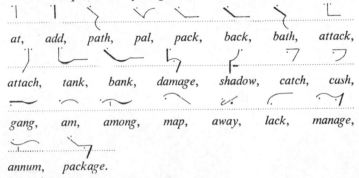

at,   add,   path,   pal,   pack,   back,   bath,   attack,

attach,   tank,   bank,   damage,   shadow,   catch,   cush,

gang,   am,   among,   map,   away,   lack,   manage,

annum,   package.

(*c*) Long *aw* is represented by a heavy dash—

saw,   paw,   ball,   bought,   talk,   tall,   auto,   chalk,

jaw,   law.

(*d*) Short *ŏ* is represented by a light dash—

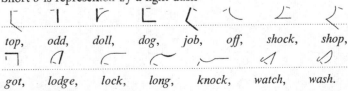

top,   odd,   doll,   dog,   job,   off,   shock,   shop,

got,   lodge,   lock,   long,   knock,   watch,   wash.

SHORT FORMS

⌣ _for,_ · _a or an,_ ＼ _of,_ ¹ _on,_ | _had._

Phrases—

∠ _on the,_ ⌐ _but the_ (the signs for _on_ and _but_ slightly slanted).

Exercise 7

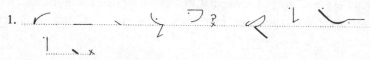

1.

2.

3.

4.

5.

6.

7.

8.

9.

10.

Exercise 8

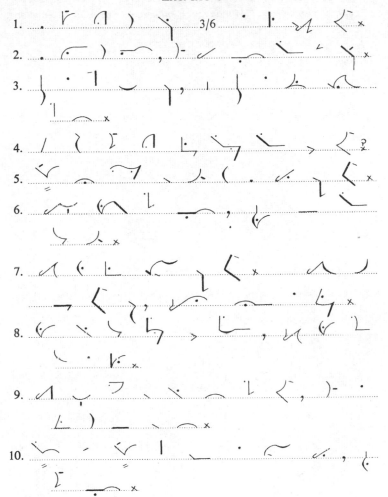

12. Second Position

When a *second-place* vowel is the *first* vowel in a word, the outline is written in *second* position, that is, the first downstroke or upstroke rests on the line—

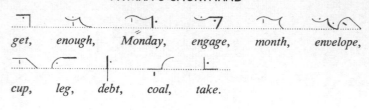

get,   enough,   Monday,   engage,   month,   envelope,

cup,   leg,   debt,   coal,   take.

Exercise 9

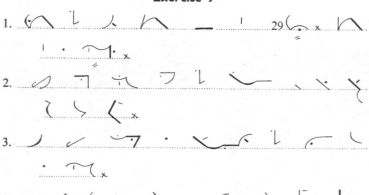

CHAPTER V

13. Third-place Vowels

The last four vowels are written in the third place. When a third-place vowel comes between two strokes, it is put in third place before the second stroke.

When a third-place vowel is the first vowel in a word, the outline is written in third position, that is, the first downstroke or upstroke is written through the line.

(*a*) Long *ē* is represented by a heavy dot—

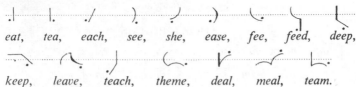

eat,   tea,   each,   see,   she,   ease,   fee,   feed,   deep,

keep,   leave,   teach,   theme,   deal,   meal,   team.

(*b*) Short *ĭ* is represented by a light dot—

if,   bit,   pick,   big,   ship,   live,   inch,   kid,   ill,

bill,   mill,   milk,   thick,   width.

(*c*) Long *ōō* is represented by a heavy dash—

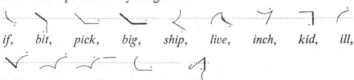

chew,   shoe,   food,   move,   youth,   tool,   pool,   cool,   tooth.

(*d*) Short *ŏŏ* is represented by a light dash—

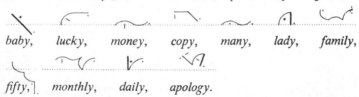

book,   took,   look,   wood,   pull,   push.

NOTE: The sound of *y* at the end of a word is represented by the light dot *ĭ*.

baby,   lucky,   money,   copy,   many,   lady,   family,

fifty,   monthly,   daily,   apology.

13

Where an outline consists only of horizontal strokes and the first vowel is a third-position vowel, the outline is written *on* the line—

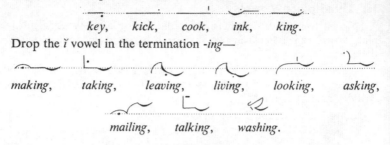

key,　　kick,　　cook,　　ink,　　king.

Drop the ĭ vowel in the termination *-ing*—

making,　　taking,　　leaving,　　living,　　looking,　　asking,

mailing,　　talking,　　washing.

SHORT FORMS

different or *difference,*　*wish,*　*put,*　*to be,*　*owe,*　*can,*　*go,*　*ought,*　*in* or *any.*

Short Form Derivatives:　*being,*　*doing,*　*having,*　*going.*

Exercise 10

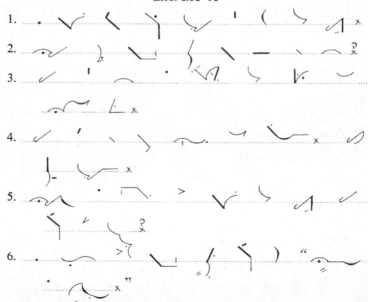

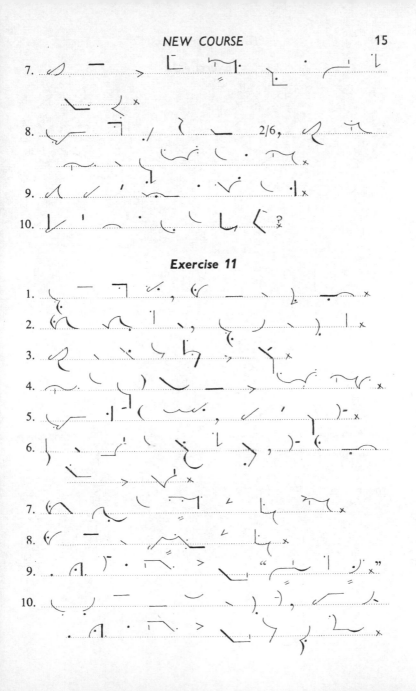

Exercise 12

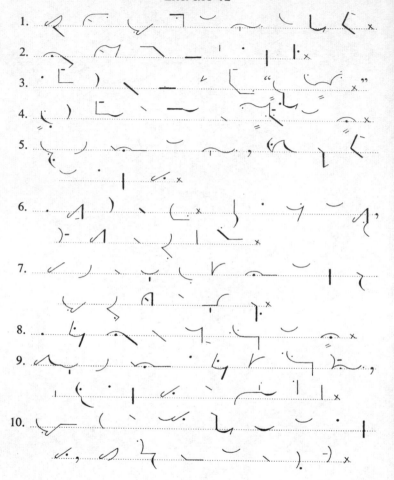

CHAPTER VI

14. Two Forms for R

Letter	Sign	Name	As in
R	↗	ray	raw, reach, carry
	↘	ar	car, air, dare

When *r* begins a word use ⟋ as in—

red, raw, road, route, rug, rush, ring, reach, ready,

readily, retail, wrong, range, rank, relief, relieve.

When a word begins with the combination "*vowel-r*" use ⟍ as in—

air, arm, or, ear, early, army.

SHORT FORMS

⟋ (up) *are*, ⟋ (up) *our* or *hour*, ⟋ (up) *and*, ⟋ (up) *should*.

NOTE: *Chay and Ray*: These strokes are somewhat similar, but they are different in slope and in the direction in which they are written. *Chay* is always written downward at a small angle from the vertical.

Ray is always written upward at a small angle from the horizontal.

For the inclusion of consonant *r* in shorthand writing, see Introduction, p. viii.

Exercise 13

1.

2.

17

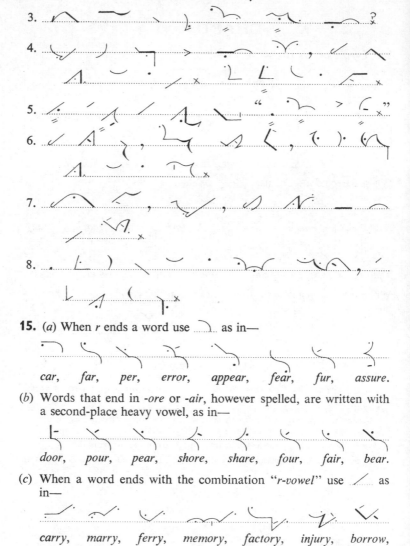

3.

4.

5.

6.

7.

8.

15. (*a*) When *r* ends a word use ⟍ as in—

car, far, per, error, appear, fear, fur, assure.

(*b*) Words that end in *-ore* or *-air*, however spelled, are written with a second-place heavy vowel, as in—

door, pour, pear, shore, share, four, fair, bear.

(*c*) When a word ends with the combination "*r-vowel*" use ╱ as in—

carry, marry, ferry, memory, factory, injury, borrow,

dairy, jury, narrow, thorough, vary, tomorrow.

SHORT FORMS

⟍ *your,* ⟍ *year,* ⟩ *whose,* / *large,* (*thank* or *thanked.*

NOTE: In the phrase *"to go"* ⟍— the vowel is inserted.

Exercise 14

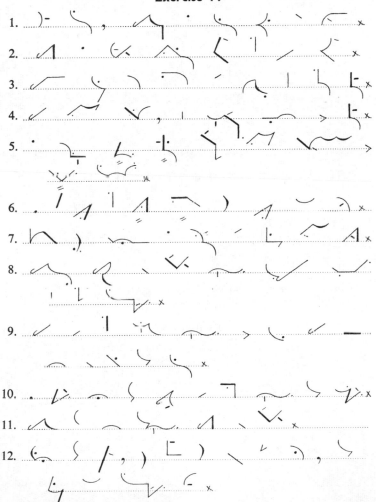

16. In order to avoid awkward joinings *r* is written—

(*a*) Downward before *m*—

room,   Rome,   remedy,   form,   firm,   alarm,   remove.

(*b*) Upward before *t, d, ch, j* and *th*—

errata,   arid,   arch,   urge,   earth.

(*c*) Upward after a straight upstroke—

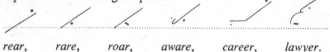

rear,   rare,   roar,   aware,   career,   lawyer.

NOTE: Usually it is better to write upward *r* in the middle of a word—

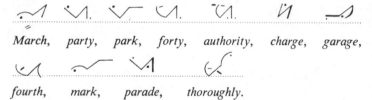

March,   party,   park,   forty,   authority,   charge,   garage,

fourth,   mark,   parade,   thoroughly.

Exercise 15

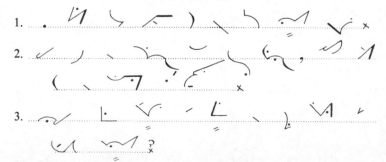

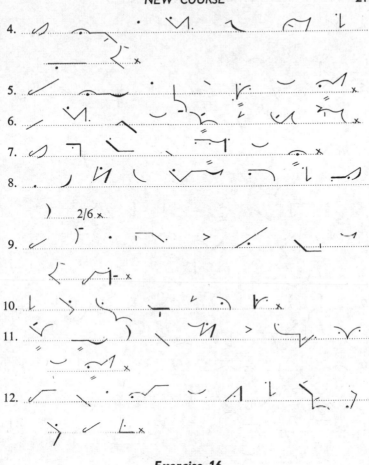

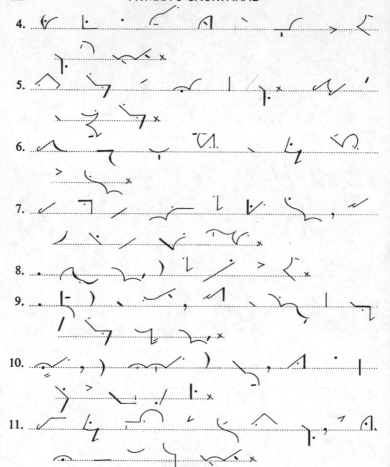

CHAPTER VII

17. Diphthongs

The four double vowels used in Pitman's Shorthand are *i*, *oi*, *ow*, and *u*, as heard in the words *I enjoy Gow's music*.

(*a*) The diphthong *i* is represented by a small angular mark written as shown, in the first vowel place—

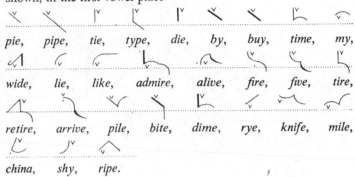

pie, pipe, tie, type, die, by, buy, time, my,

wide, lie, like, admire, alive, fire, five, tire,

retire, arrive, pile, bite, dime, rye, knife, mile,

china, shy, ripe.

(*b*) The diphthong *oi* is written as shown, in the first vowel place—

boy, joy, enjoy, toy, boil, boiler, annoy, coil,

toll, coy, alloy.

(*c*) The diphthong *ow* is written as shown, in the third vowel place—

cow, out, loud, mouth, row, couch, outlay, lounge, county.

(*d*) The diphthong *u* is represented by a small semicircle written in the third vowel place—

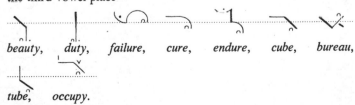

beauty, duty, failure, cure, endure, cube, bureau,

tube, occupy.

SHORT FORMS

ˇ I or eye, ∧ how, ∟ why, ∩ beyond, ⌒ you, ᴄ with, ᴄ when,
ᴐ what, ⌐ would, ⌒ me, ‿ owing.

Exercise 17

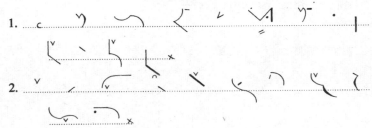

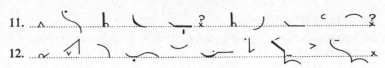

11.

12.

Exercise 18

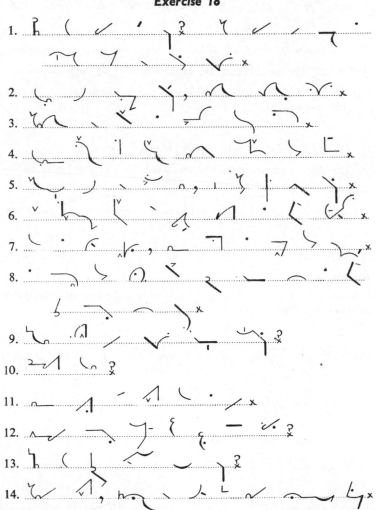

1.

2.

3.

4.

5.

6.

7.

8.

9.

10.

11.

12.

13.

14.

18. Joined Diphthongs

(*a*) The diphthong signs are joined to strokes when an easy joining can be made—

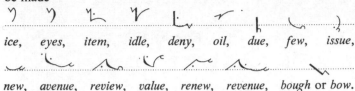

ice,   eyes,   item,   idle,   deny,   oil,   due,   few,   issue,

new,   avenue,   review,   value,   renew,   revenue,   bough or bow.

(*b*) The sign for *ow* is contracted in the word ⌇ *now*.

(*c*) The sign for *i* is contracted before *l, m, k,* and upward *r* to form such phrases as—

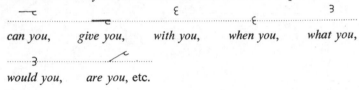

I will (I'll),   I am (I'm),   I may,   I can,   I write.

(*d*) The short form *you* is turned on its side to form the phrases—

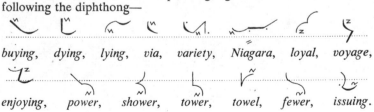

can you,   give you,   with you,   when you,   what you,

would you,   are you, etc.

19. Triphones

A small tick added to a diphthong sign indicates another vowel following the diphthong—

buying,   dying,   lying,   via,   variety,   Niagara,   loyal,   voyage,

enjoying,   power,   shower,   tower,   towel,   fewer,   issuing.

Exercise 19

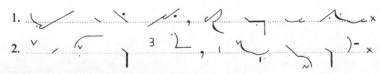

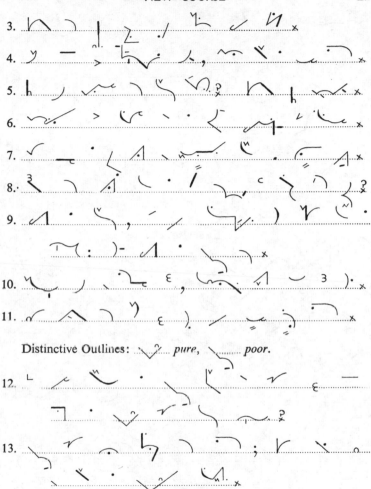

Distinctive Outlines: *pure,* *poor.*

Exercise 20

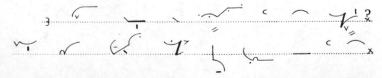

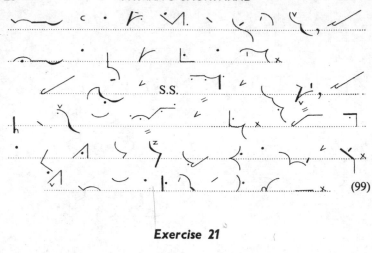

(99)

Exercise 21

(122)

20. Consonant H

Letter	Sign	Name	As in
H		hay	he, high, hay
		hay	hope, happy, head

(a) When *h* is the only consonant stroke, or is followed by *k* or *g*, use the downward form—

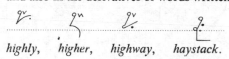

he,   hay,   high,   hake,   Haig,

and also in the derivatives of words written with the downward *h*—

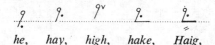

highly,   higher,   highway,   haystack.

(b) Use the upward form when *h* is joined to other consonants—

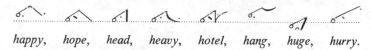

happy,   hope,   head,   heavy,   hotel,   hang,   huge,   hurry.

(c) The word *hope* is contracted to the stroke *p* to form the phrases

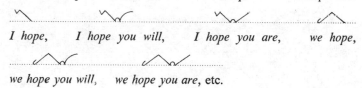

I hope,   I hope you will,   I hope you are,   we hope,

we hope you will,   we hope you are, etc.

(d) The word *he* is represented in the middle or at the end of a phrase by the short form ___ı___ In other cases ___ſ___ is used.

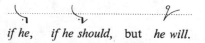

if he,   if he should,   but   he will.

Exercise 22

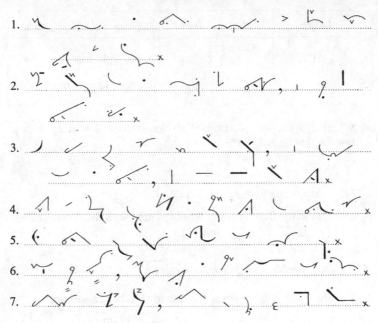

Exercise 23

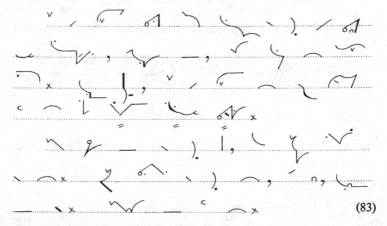

(83)

CHAPTER VIII

21. *S* Circle

The very frequently occurring consonant *s*, and its corresponding heavy sound *z*, are represented by a small circle as well as by the strokes ⟩ and ⟩.

The small circle joins easily to other consonant strokes at the beginning, in the middle, or at the end of a word. At the beginning of a word, the *s* circle is always read first; at the end of a word, the *s* circle is always read last.

The *s* circle is written inside a curve—

(a) *face, these, shoes, loss, knows, names, bills,*

else, anxious, less, months, leaves, shows, lose,

miss, arms, ears, nice, size, voice, invoice,

announce, advice, news, views, refuse, items,

issues, errors, forms, office, affairs.

(b) *safe, seem, slow, song, silk, sir, small,*

Sunday, sense, sale, sales, save, saving, sell,

selling, sleep, snow, some, soon, sun, since,

similar, soil, south, sign, salary.

(c) *message, absence, business, cousin, reason, receive,*

31

receiving,   passing,   dozen,   inside,   music,   Wednesday.

SHORT FORMS

° *has* or *as*, *his* or *is*, *several*, *those*, *this*, *thus*.

NOTE: *has the* or *as the*, *is the*.

Exercise 24

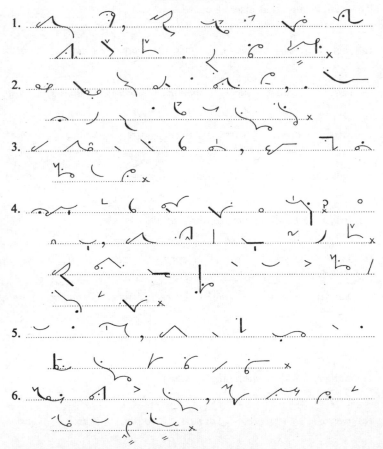

7.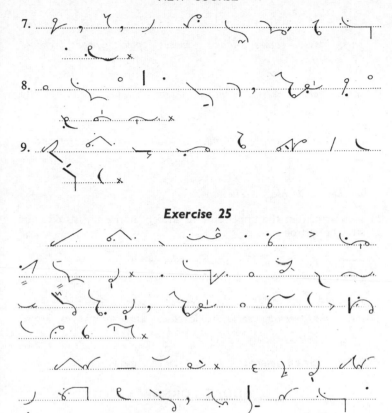

8.

9.

Exercise 25

(113)

22. The *s* circle is written with a left (anti-clockwise) motion to straight strokes.

(*a*) This means that it is written on the right side of straight down-strokes—

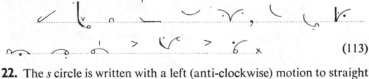

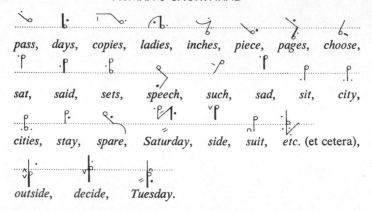

pass, days, copies, ladies, inches, piece, pages, choose,

sat, said, sets, speech, such, sad, sit, city,

cities, stay, spare, Saturday, side, suit, etc. (et cetera),

outside, decide, Tuesday.

(b) It is written on the upper side of straight horizontal strokes and straight upstrokes—

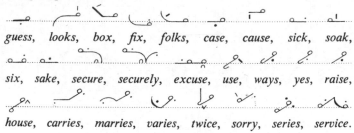

guess, looks, box, fix, folks, case, cause, sick, soak,

six, sake, secure, securely, excuse, use, ways, yes, raise,

house, carries, marries, varies, twice, sorry, series, service.

SHORT FORMS

because, special or specially, speak,

subject or subjected.

The *s* circle is added to short forms—

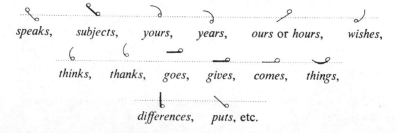

speaks, subjects, yours, years, ours or hours, wishes,

thinks, thanks, goes, gives, comes, things,

differences, puts, etc.

Exercise 26

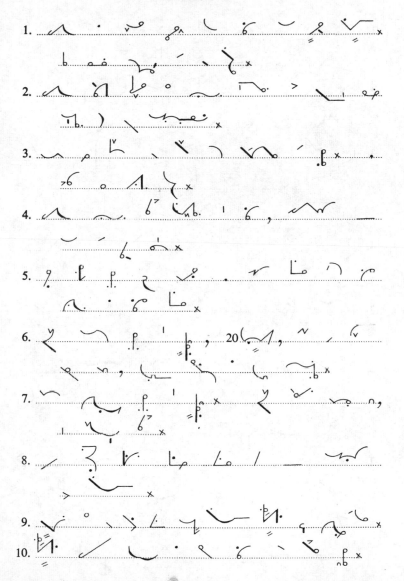

Exercise 27

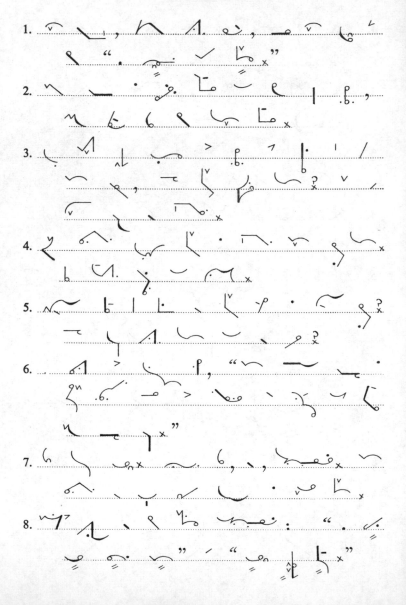

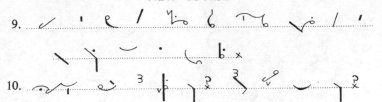

9.

10.

23. Final *s* circle represents the word *us* in such phrases as—

for us,   to us,   give us,   take us,   show us,   making us,

charge us, etc.

NOTE: *with us*,   *when is*,   *when is the*,   *what is*,

what is the.

Exercise 28

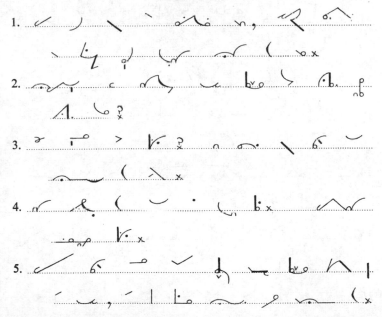

1.

2.

3.

4.

5.

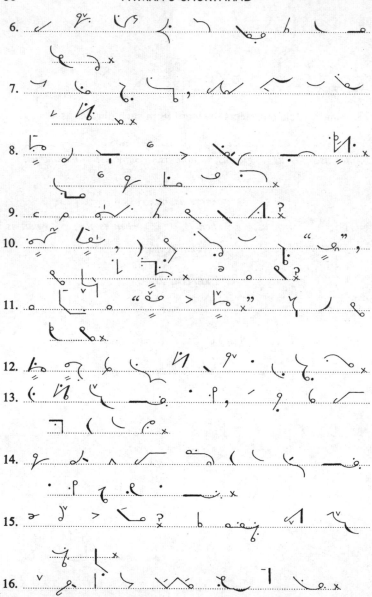

24. The *s* circle is written on the outside of the angle formed by two straight strokes—

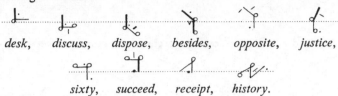

desk,   discuss,   dispose,   besides,   opposite,   justice,

sixty,   succeed,   receipt,   history.

25. The circle at the beginning of a word represents *s* only.

In the few words beginning with *z*, the stroke *z* is used—

zeal,   zero,   zenith, etc.

Exercise 29

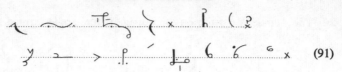

 (91)

26. Upward *r* is used following the curve and circle in words like—

officer,   answer,   sincere,

even though the words do not end with a vowel; because a much more swiftly written and readable outline is obtained in this way. (See p. 18.)

27. The stroke *l* may easily be written downward, and when it precedes or follows circle *s* attached to a curve it is written in the same direction as the circle—

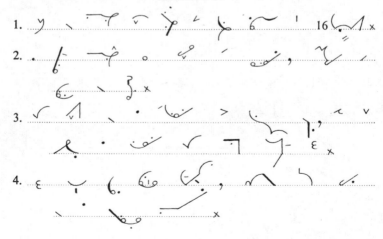

vessel, nicely, cancel, council, lesson, noiseless, muscle, loosely.

Exercise 30

CHAPTER IX

28. St Loop

(a) A small loop, written in the same direction as the *s* circle, represents *st* (called "stee")—

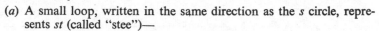

fast, missed, must, honest, assist, list, invoiced, announced,

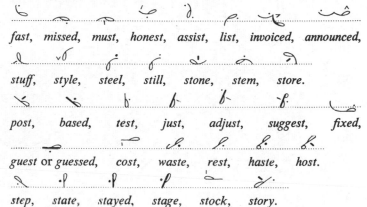

stuff, style, steel, still, stone, stem, store.

post, based, test, just, adjust, suggest, fixed,

guest or guessed, cost, waste, rest, haste, host.

step, state, stayed, stage, stock, story.

(b) The *st* loop represents either a light or heavy final sound—

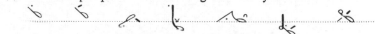

past, paused, used, advised, refused, disposed, supposed.

Final *s* circle after a *st* loop is added as shown—

lists, posts, tests, wastes, adjusts, costs, suggests.

(c) The *st* loop may be written in the middle of a word—

testing, adjusting, suggesting, artistic.

SHORT FORMS

first, most, influence, influenced, next, all, though.

NOTE: although, all right, already, always, almost, also, as fast as.

41

Exercise 31

Distinctive Outlines:  cost, caused.

1.

2.

3.

4.

5.

6.

7.

8.

9.

10.

11.

12.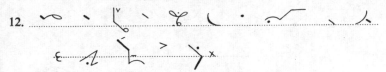

29. Str Loop

A large final loop, written in the same direction as the *s* circle, represents *ster*—

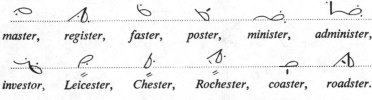

master,   register,   faster,   poster,   minister,   administer,

investor,   Leicester,   Chester,   Rochester,   coaster,   roadster.

The *ster* loop is not used at the beginning of a word.

The *s* circle is added for such words as—

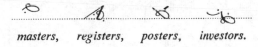

masters,   registers,   posters,   investors.

Exercise 32

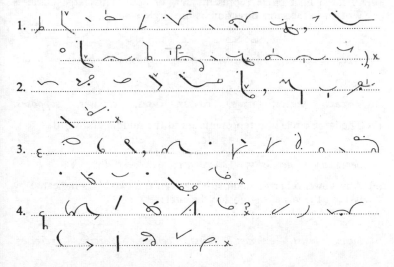

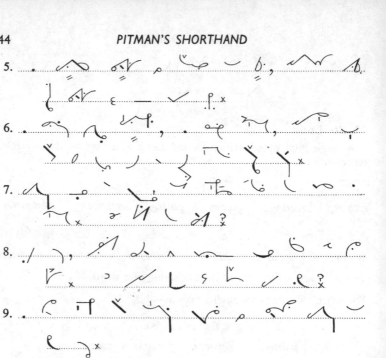

30. Ses Circle

(a) A large final circle represents *ses*, or *sez*. This large circle is written in the same direction as the circle *s*—

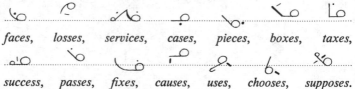

faces,   losses,   services,   cases,   pieces,   boxes,   taxes,

success,   passes,   fixes,   causes,   uses,   chooses,   supposes.

(b) The large circle also represents *ses* in the middle of a word—

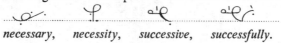

necessary,   necessity,   successive,   successfully.

(c) Any vowel other than short *ĕ* between the two *s's* is indicated by writing the vowel sign inside the circle—

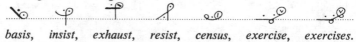

basis,   insist,   exhaust,   resist,   census,   exercise,   exercises.

SHORT FORMS

ᔦ _themselves,_ ᑫ _ourselves,_ ○ _as is,_ ○ _is as,_ ⌒ _myself,_
⌒ᑌ _himself,_ ᑭ _itself,_ / _much._

Exercise 33

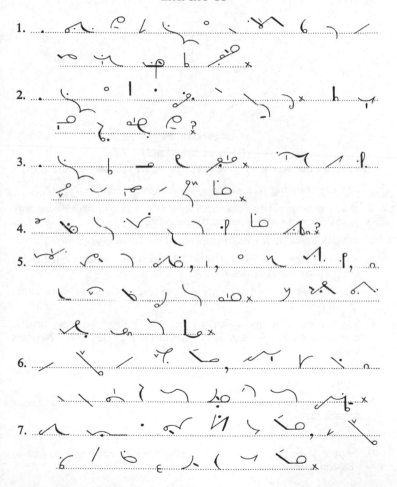

8.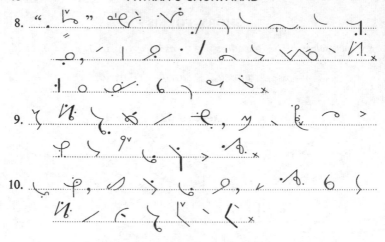

9.

10.

Exercise 34

(*Write in Shorthand*)

(*Phrases are indicated by hyphens. Short Forms are indicated by italic type.*)

1. *Are-you* enjoying *your* study *of-this subject*? *I-hope-you-are.*

2. *When you-can* write these exercises fast, *you*-will-*be on-your* way *to*-making *your* living *in a* business office.

3. Besides *its* value *to-you*, *I-hope-you* like-*the subject for-itself.*

4. *As you* know, *this subject is* widely used *in* business offices, *but it-has* many uses besides *this.*

5. *You-can* use *it for*-many *different* purposes. *Can-you* name some *of-them*?

6. *The* success *of*-many *a* famous head *of a large* business firm *is* due *to-his* study *of-this subject. It-was-the first* step *in-his* business career.

7. Write-*the* signs *as-fast-as you-can.* *Al*ways read back *what you*-write.

8. Each time *you*-write an exercise *you-should* write *it* faster *and* read *it* back faster.

9. Write-*the* forms just-*as* they appear *in-this* book.

10. *In*-time *you*-may, if-*you wish*, write these same forms *as-fast-as you-can speak.*

31. Sw Circle

(a) A large initial circle represents *sw* (called "sway"). The *sw* circle is written in the same direction as the *s* circle—

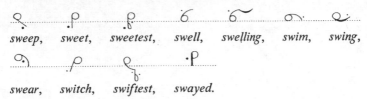

sweep, sweet, sweetest, swell, swelling, swim, swing,

swear, switch, swiftest, swayed.

(b) The *sw* circle represents the words *as we* in such phrases as—

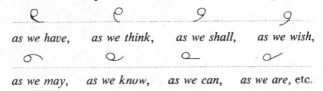

as we have, as we think, as we shall, as we wish,

as we may, as we know, as we can, as we are, etc.

It is also used to form the phrase $\quad$ as well as.

(c) The large circle represents the two *s*'s in such phrases as—

this is, this is the, this city, as soon as, as soon as possible.

SHORT FORMS

United States, New York, largest.

Special Phrase: United States of America.

Exercise 35

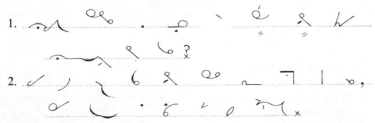

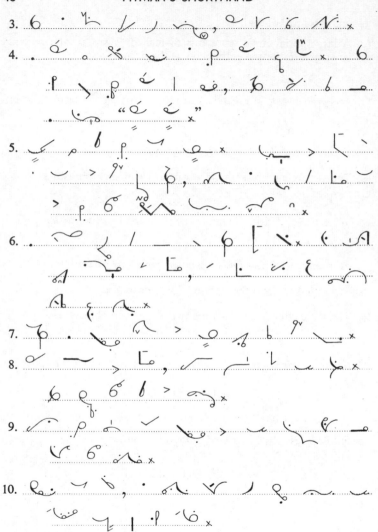

32. Vowel Indication

(*a*) A circle or loop is always read first at the beginning of a word. When a vowel begins a word, we must write a stroke in order to place the initial vowel sign—

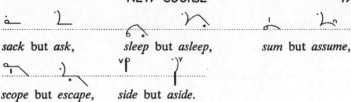

sack but *ask*,   sleep but *asleep*,   sum but *assume*,

scope but *escape*,   side but *aside*.

(b) A circle or loop is always read last at the end of a word. When a word ends in a vowel, we must write a stroke in order to place the final vowel sign—

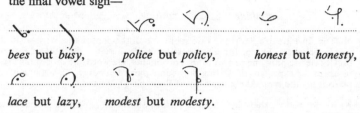

bees but *busy*,   police but *policy*,   honest but *honesty*,

lace but *lazy*,   modest but *modesty*.

(c) When a vowel occurs between *s* and *t*, the *st* loop is not used—

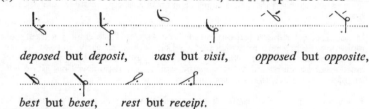

deposed but *deposit*,   vast but *visit*,   opposed but *opposite*,

best but *beset*,   rest but *receipt*.

The outline thus indicates the presence or absence of a vowel sound.

(d) As there are no places alongside a circle or loop for placing vowel signs, we must write—

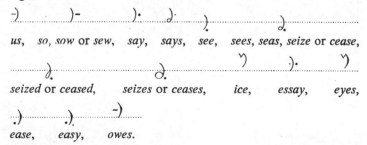

us,   so, sow or *sew*,   say,   says,   see,   sees, seas, seize or *cease*,

seized or *ceased*,   seizes or *ceases*,   ice,   essay,   eyes,

ease,   easy,   owes.

Special Phrases: ⟍ *so much,* ⟍ *too much,* ⟍ *how much,* ⟍ *as much as,* ⟍ *inasmuch as,* ⟍ *as much as possible,* ⟍ *as early as possible,* ⟍ *as far as possible.*

SHORT FORMS

⟍ *especial* or *especially,* ⟍ *language* or *owing,* ⟍ *young,* ⟍ *anything,* ⟍ *nothing,* ⟍ *something.*

NOTE: In Pitman's Shorthand we represent all the consonants we hear in the words we write. Except for the "short forms," where for the sake of extreme brevity we use only one or two of the consonants in a word, we do not normally resort to the expedient of writing only some part of a word. This is one of the reasons for the remarkable legibility of Pitman's Shorthand.

As we proceed we shall find that the various abbreviating devices of the system enable us to represent all the consonants in words in concise, legible, and rapid shorthand forms. These outlines are so clearly distinctive that it is unnecessary to insert the vowel signs. The outlines are perfectly legible without them.

In addition to writing a full outline of the consonants, we employ a means of indicating the presence or absence of a vowel with very nearly every abbreviating device of the system. Another expedient, highly prized by the fastest and most accurate shorthand writers in the world, is position writing. It is not surprising, therefore, that the system is so legible.

From now on we shall omit all but essential vowel signs in the shorthand exercises; but we shall take care to insert essential vowels to eliminate any possibility of hesitation in reading back shorthand notes.

Exercise 36

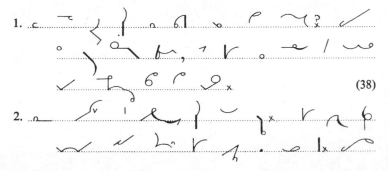

1.

(38)

2.

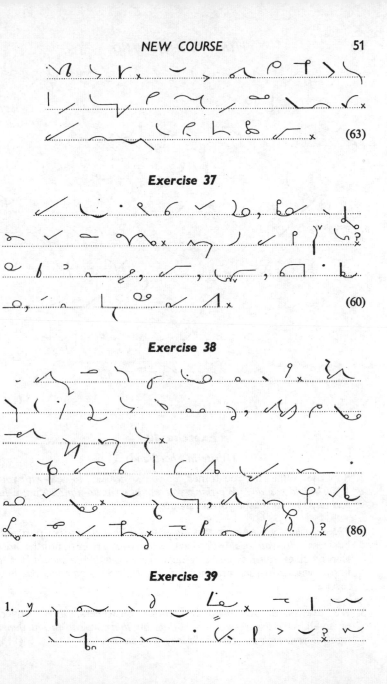

(63)

Exercise 37

(60)

Exercise 38

(86)

Exercise 39

1.

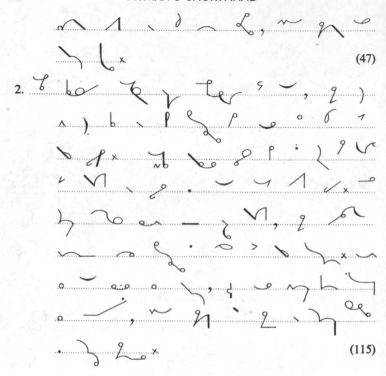

(47)

2.

(115)

Exercise 40

(*Write in Shorthand*)

1. Suppose some big customer *of-yours* ceased *to-*deal-with-you.
What-would you do? *We-think-you* would write *to-him*, asking if-*he*
had any *special* reason *for-his* silence.

2. *This-is* what *we-are-*now asking-*you*. *Although in-the* past *our*
business *with-you in-this-*city *was* extensive, *several* months *have*
elapsed since *you* last *had any* dealings *with*-us. *We should* like *to*
know *why*, *as-we-are* unaware *of any* failure *to-give-you-the* best
service.

3. *We a*lways desire *to-*satisfy *all-our* customers, *large* buyers
or small. *We* assure-*you we-shall-do anything we-can* to put *things*
right, if-*you think our* service *in-any-*way faulty.   (118)

Exercise 41

(*Write in Shorthand*)

1. *I-have*-seen *your* notice *in to*-day's "Star," *and-I should*-like *to-have* details *of-your* new Masters' Reading Series. *I-think* such *a* series *should* make *a* wide appeal, *and-I-wish-you much* success *with-it*.

2. Many *of-those who have*-seen my set *of* "Stories *of-the* Earth, Sea, *and* Sky" *speak* highly *of-it*, *and-several*, *I*-know, *have* bought similar sets *for-themselves*.

3. *I*-am-sorry *you have* allowed "Poster Designing" *to*-go out *of* stock. Such *a* book, *it*-seems *to-me*, *should-have a large* sale, *as* so-many *are*-now taking-up-*the* study *of-this-subject*. *In*-view *of-this*, may *I* suggest *a* new issue? (116)

CHAPTER X

33. Halving

Strokes are halved to indicate a following *t* or *d*.

(*a*) In words of one *syllable* a light stroke is generally halved to indicate a following *t* but not a following *d*—

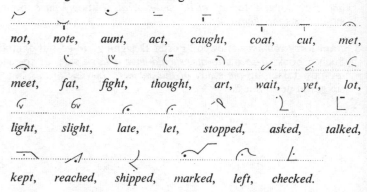

not, note, aunt, act, caught, coat, cut, met,

meet, fat, fight, thought, art, wait, yet, lot,

light, slight, late, let, stopped, asked, talked,

kept, reached, shipped, marked, left, checked.

NOTE: ⁓ *night*.

The *s* circle is always read last: ⚭ *notes*, ⚬ *acts*, ⚬ *thoughts*,

⚬ *lots*, ⚬ *waits*, ⚬ *nights*.

(*b*) In words of one *syllable* a heavy stroke is generally halved to indicate a following *d* but not a following *t*—

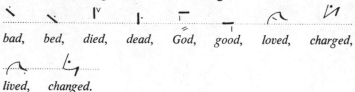

bad, bed, died, dead, God, good, loved, charged,

lived, changed.

SHORT FORMS

— *quite*, — *could*, ⟨ *that*, ⟨ *without*, ⚬ *sent*, ⌡ *wished*.

Exercise 42

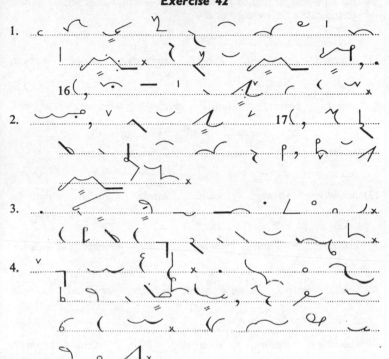

Exercise 43

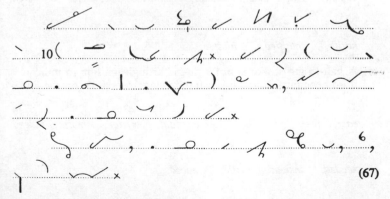

(67)

34. (*a*) In words of two or more syllables, a stroke is generally halved to indicate a following *t* or *d*—

(1) *attached,   answered,   except,   suggested,   avoid,   market,*

recent,   absent,   admit,   arrived,   engaged,   enjoyed,

estate,   stated,   exact,   result,   benefit,   booklet.

(2) *actually,   writing,   badly,   lately,   entire,   entirely,*

evidence,   sometimes,   waiting,   certain,   goodbye,   absolutely.

(3) *omit,   omitted,   note,   noted,   accept,   accepted,   submit,*

submitted,   await,   awaited,   limit,   limited,   visit,

visited,   list,   listed,   remit,   remitted,   deduct,   deducted,

notify,   notified,   invited.

(*b*) A half-length stroke is not written through the line to indicate a third position. Words like the following are written on the line—

east,   feet,   fit,   sheets,   bid,   did,   written,   invite,   indeed,

needed,   instead,   little,   moved.

(c) Where a final diphthong is joined, a single stroke is generally halved to indicate a final *t* or *d*—

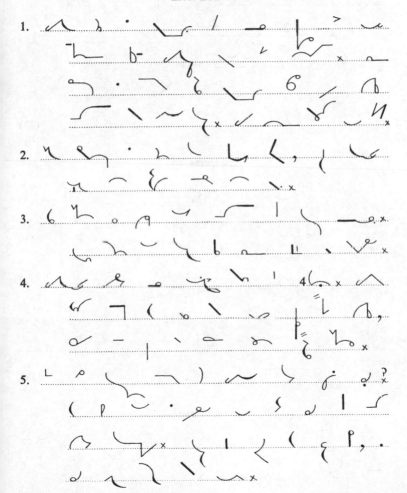

doubt,   about,   bowed,   cute,   issued.

Exercise 44

1.

2.

3.

4.

5.

Exercise 45

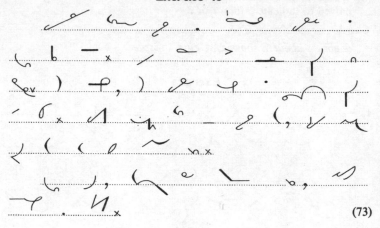

(73)

Exercise 46

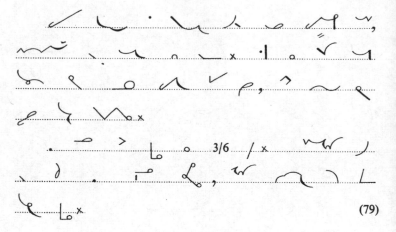

(79)

Exercise 47

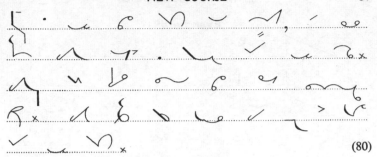

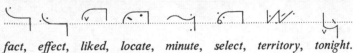

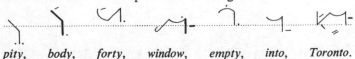

(80)

Exercise 48

(*Write in Shorthand*)

We-have-sent several notes *to-you* asking-*you* to pay-*the* bill *for-the*-goods *you* bought six-months-ago, *but-you* have-not answered *any of-them*.

We-are-sorry *to* say *that* now *we-shall-have* to-take-*the usual* steps *to*-avoid-*the* loss *of-our* money, if-*your* cheque *is*-not received by-*the first of next* month. *We* urge *you* to-mail *your* cheque *to*-us *without*-delay.
(74)

35. (*a*) To avoid confusion with *should* and *and*, we do not use *rt* and *rts* standing alone. Therefore we write—

rate, rates, right, rights, write, wrote, route.

(*b*) In certain words, where the proper length of a halved stroke would not clearly show, the halving principle is not employed—

fact, effect, liked, locate, minute, select, territory, tonight.

(*c*) When a final vowel follows *t* or *d*, it is necessary to write the stroke *t* or *d* in order to place the vowel sign—

pity, body, forty, window, empty, into, Toronto.

Exercise 49

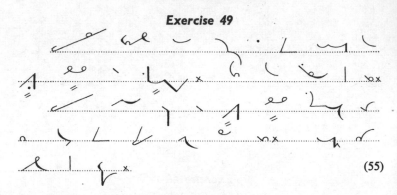

(55)

Exercise 50

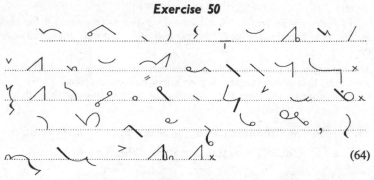

(64)

Exercise 51

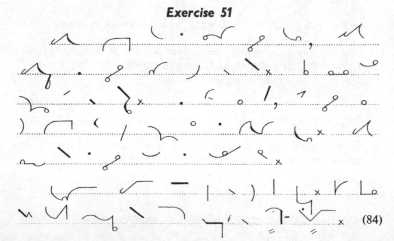

(84)

Exercise 52

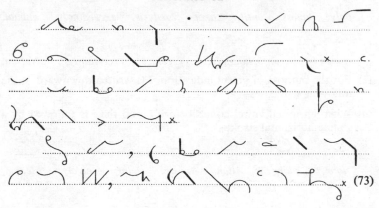

(73)

Exercise 53

(*Write in Shorthand*)

Do-you know *that-we* sell good tyres? *It-is*-not-necessary *for-you* to buy tyres *in a* repair shop, *for our* store now carries *them*. *You-can* buy *them* when *you-are in-the* store, just-*as you would* select silks, or *something for-your* house.

These tyres *are* good value, *and*-they sell rapidly. Each *of-them* carries *our* guarantee. (63)

Exercise 54

(*Write in Shorthand*)

It-is quite some time since *you* bought *anything in-this* store. *I*-am-writing *to-you myself*, *because I should-be* sorry *to*-lose *your* custom.

It-may-*be that-we-have* offended *you in*-some-way. If-*this-is-the* case, *I*-hope-*you*-will write *to-me*. *Our* service *and our* way *of-do*ing business *are things which-we* boast about. *It-would-be a* pity *to* stay away *because of-something which could-be* easily remedied, *and you-should*-not hesitate *to*-write *to-me and* let-*me*-know-*the* cause. (95)

36. Downward L

Usually *l* is written upward.

(1) For convenience, *l* is usually written downward after *n* or *ng*—

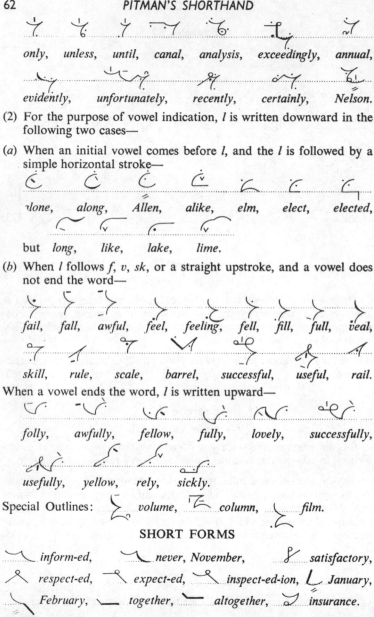

only, unless, until, canal, analysis, exceedingly, annual,

evidently, unfortunately, recently, certainly, Nelson.

(2) For the purpose of vowel indication, *l* is written downward in the following two cases—

(*a*) When an initial vowel comes before *l*, and the *l* is followed by a simple horizontal stroke—

alone, along, Allen, alike, elm, elect, elected,

but *long, like, lake, lime.*

(*b*) When *l* follows *f, v, sk,* or a straight upstroke, and a vowel does not end the word—

fail, fall, awful, feel, feeling, fell, fill, full, veal,

skill, rule, scale, barrel, successful, useful, rail.

When a vowel ends the word, *l* is written upward—

folly, awfully, fellow, fully, lovely, successfully,

usefully, yellow, rely, sickly.

Special Outlines: *volume,* *column,* *film.*

SHORT FORMS

inform-ed, *never, November,* *satisfactory,*

respect-ed, *expect-ed,* *inspect-ed-ion,* *January,*

February, *together,* *altogether,* *insurance.*

Exercise 55

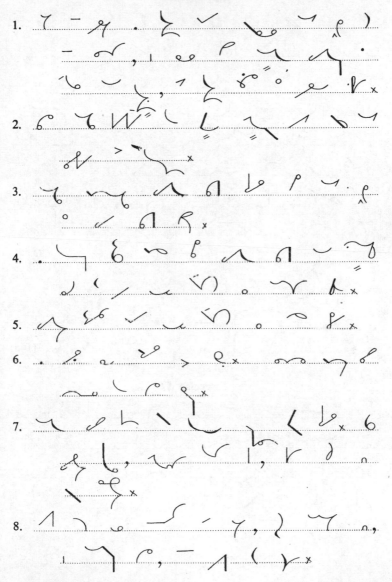

Exercise 56

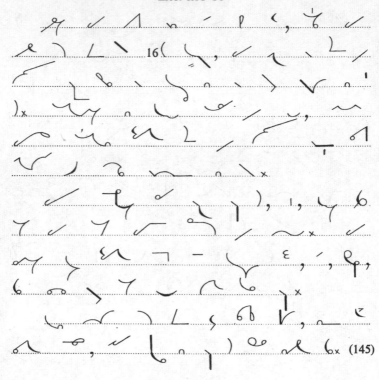

Exercise 57

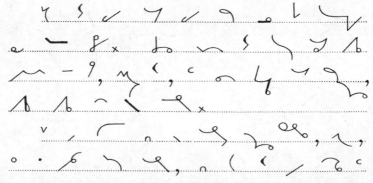

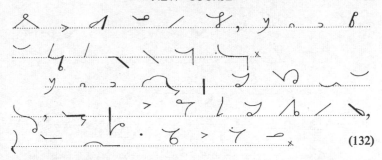

(132)

37. Abbreviated W

A small initial semicircle, written as shown, is used as an abbreviation for *w* at the beginning of *k, g, m,* and upward and downward *r*—

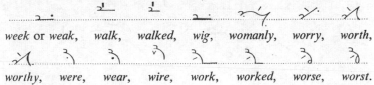

week or *weak,* *walk,* *walked,* *wig,* *womanly,* *worry,* *worth,*

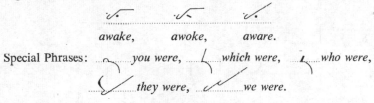

worthy, *were,* *wear,* *wire,* *work,* *worked,* *worse,* *worst.*

NOTE: The small semicircle is always read first. When a vowel begins a word, the stroke *w* must be written—

awake, *awoke,* *aware.*

Special Phrases: *you were,* *which were,* *who were,* *they were,* *we were.*

Exercise 58

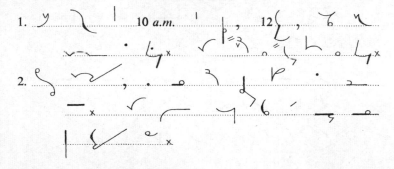

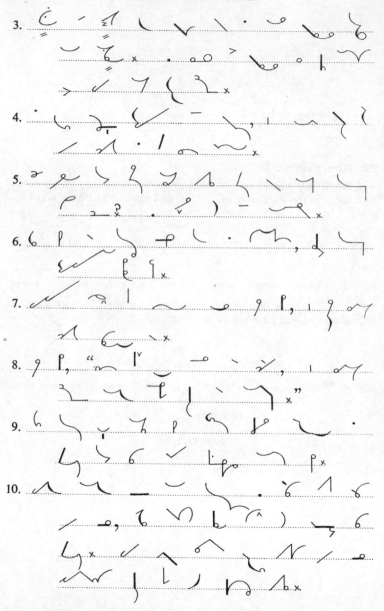

Exercise 59

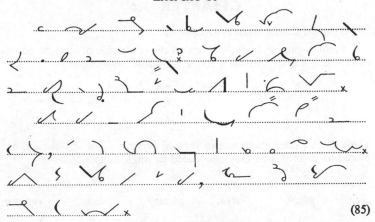

(85)

Exercise 60

(*Write in Shorthand*)

I-wish to-thank-you for-the catalogue *which-you*-were good-enough *to* post *to-me* recently. *Several* books listed *on* page 21 appear *to-be* just *what I*-am looking *for*. *I-have* marked *them on-the* attached sheet.

Although I-think that-these books *should-be* useful *to-me in*-my work, *I should* like *to inspect them to* see if-they *would-be satisfactory*. May *any of-the* books *be sent* back *to-you* if, *when I-have* looked at-*them*, *I*-decide *that*-they *would*-not-*be satisfactory for*-my purpose?   (96)

CHAPTER XI

38. Double Consonants—*Pl Series*

A small beginning hook, written on the circle side of straight down-strokes and *k* and *g*, forms a series of double consonants—

pl,   bl,   tl,   dl,   chl,   jl,   kl,   gl.

These double consonants are called *pel, bel,* etc. The vowel signs are placed to them just as they are placed to single consonants—

play,   place,   places,   placing,   placed,   replace,

plate,   played,   plus,   blue,   black,   blame,   blank,

block,   class,   clear,   clerk,   close,   closed,   enclose,

cloth,   clothes,   club,   claim,   glass,   glad,   single,

apply,   applied,   replied,   simple,   couple,   able,   enable,

double,   table,   reasonable,   terrible,   oblige,   total,

entitled,   include,   included,   including,   local,   uncle,

article,   duplicate,   o'clock.

Distinctive Outlines: valuable,   available.

An *s* circle is written inside the hook of the *pl* series—

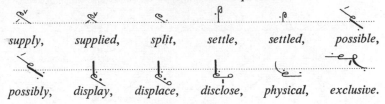

supply,   supplied,   split,   settle,   settled,   possible,

possibly,   display,   displace,   disclose,   physical,   exclusive.

SHORT FORMS

people,   *belief, believe* or *believed*,   *tell*,   *till*,

deliver, delivered or *delivery*,   *call*,   *called*,   *equal*
or *equally*,   *equalled* or *cold*,   *build* or *building* (or *able-to*).

Phrases: *at all*,   *by all*,   *I believe*,   *able to*.

Exercise 61

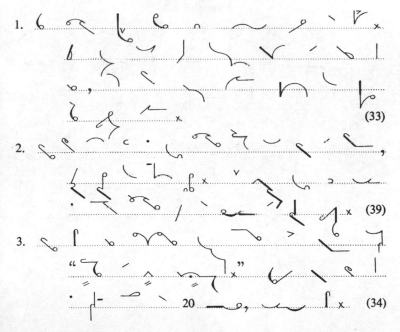

1.   (33)

2.   (39)

3.   20   (34)

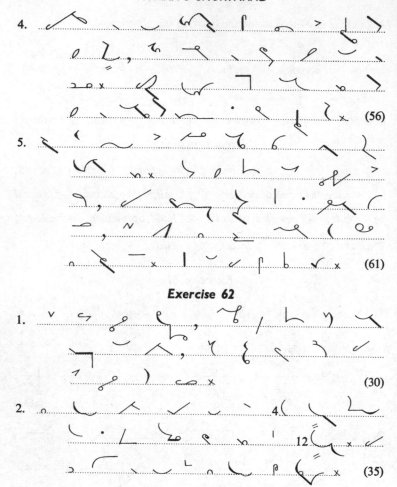

4.   (56)

5.   (61)

Exercise 62

1.   (30)

2.   (35)

3.   (46)

4.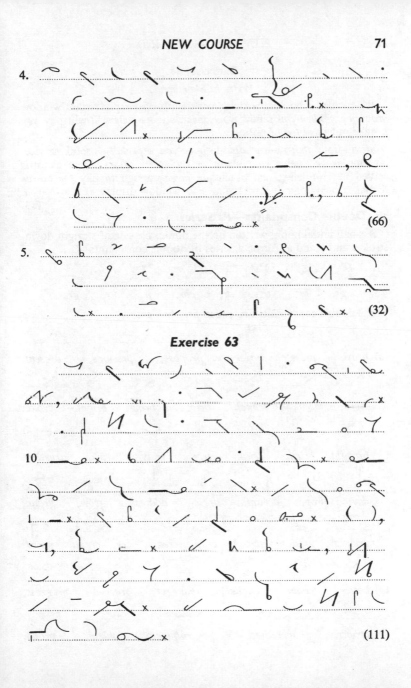

(66)

5.

(32)

Exercise 63

10

(111)

Exercise 64

(*Write in Shorthand*)

We-enclose *a* booklet *which gives* details *of-our* plate-glass window *insurance*. *When-you* renew *your insurance we-believe it*-will pay *you to*-take-out *this* type *of* policy.

You-will-note *that-we-are able-to give-you especially* useful service. *As*-soon-*as-we* receive *your* claim *we* replace-*the* glass. *Your* claim *is* settled *without*-delay, *and a* cheque *large* enough *to* pay *for all-the* damage, including *any* damage *to-your* window display, *is* sent *to-you*.

(83)

39. Double Consonants—*Pr Series*

A small initial hook, written on the non-circle side of straight down-strokes and *k* and *g*, forms a series of double consonants—

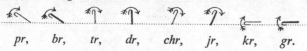

pr,   br,   tr,   dr,   chr,   jr,   kr,   gr.

These double consonants are called *per*, *ber*, etc.

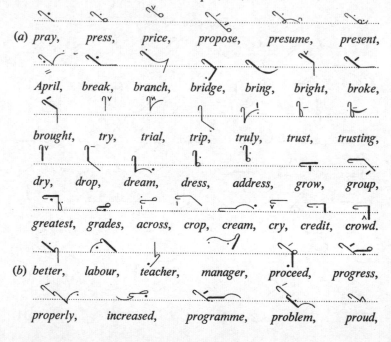

(a) *pray,   press,   price,   propose,   presume,   present,*

April,   break,   branch,   bridge,   bring,   bright,   broke,

brought,   try,   trial,   trip,   truly,   trust,   trusting,

dry,   drop,   dream,   dress,   address,   grow,   group,

greatest,   grades,   across,   crop,   cream,   cry,   credit,   crowd.

(b) *better,   labour,   teacher,   manager,   proceed,   progress,*

properly,   increased,   programme,   problem,   proud,

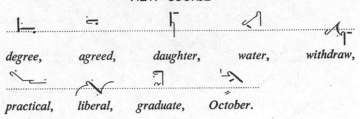

degree,   agreed,   daughter,   water,   withdraw,

practical,   liberal,   graduate,   October.

SHORT FORMS

Dr., doctor,   dear,   during,   truth,   principal, principally or principle,   liberty,   member, remember or remembered,   number or numbered,   chair,   cheer,   care.

Exercise 65

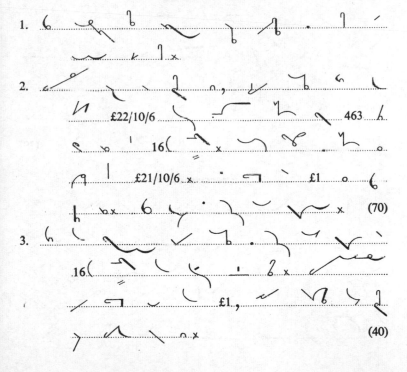

1.

2.   £22/10/6   463   16   £21/10/6   £1   (70)

3.   16   £1,   (40)

4.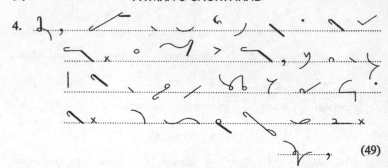

(49)

Exercise 66

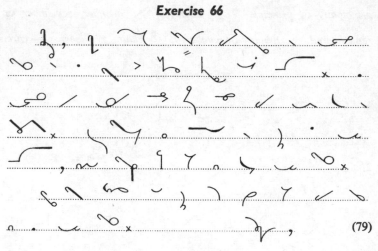

(79)

Exercise 67

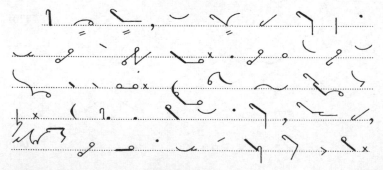

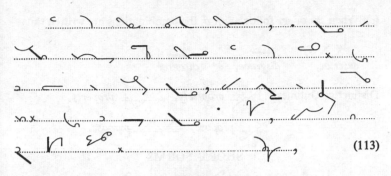

(113)

Exercise 68

(*Write in Shorthand*)

Dear Dr. Waters, *We-are* taking-*the liberty of* asking-*you to* address *our* graduates *on*-Monday, 29th-*January. Our principal and* teachers, *as*-well-*as-the* graduates, *would-be* proud *to-have-you deliver an* address. *We-know-that what-you-would tell*-us *as-the principal* speaker *on-our* programme *would-be remembered* by-*all our* graduates *for*-many-*years to-come.*

We-know-*that-you have* many *calls to-speak, and-that your* time *is* exceedingly valuable, *but-we*-feel *that-you*-will-be-glad *to*-talk *to*-us if-*you* possibly *can. We*-trust *that-you*-will-*be-able-to* accept. *Yours*-truly, (107)

40. (*a*) When an initial circle or loop is written on the same side as the hook of the *pr* series, the *r* is included—

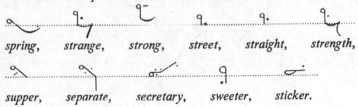

spring,   strange,   strong,   street,   straight,   strength,

supper,   separate,   secretary,   sweeter,   sticker.

(*b*) Both hook and circle are shown in the middle of a word—

extra,   extremely,   industry,   district,   express.

(c) When *skr* or *sgr* follows *t* or *d*, the combinations are written thus—

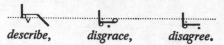

describe,   *disgrace*,   *disagree*.

Distinctive Outlines: *propriety*,   *property*,

propose,   *purpose*.

SHORT FORMS

description,   *surprise*,   *surprised*.

Exercise 69

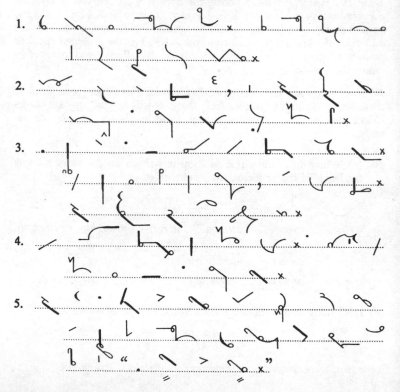

Exercise 70

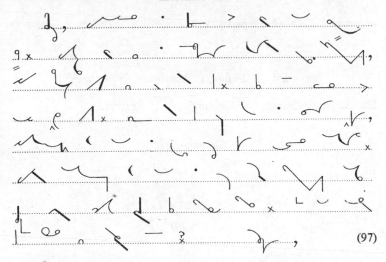

(97)

41. Special Use of Double Consonants

In a special group of words, the double consonant strokes are used although a distinct vowel comes between a consonant and hook *l* or hook *r*. The double consonant strokes are employed in order to secure briefer or more facile outlines. The most important of these words are given below.

Although it is seldom necessary to vocalize these special outlines, a dot vowel may be indicated by writing a small circle instead of the dot, either after or before the double consonant stroke—

parcel,   darling,   dark,   charm,   direct,   directly.

The short *ĕ* vowel is never indicated in words like *person,*
girl,   term.

A dash vowel, or a diphthong, is shown by writing the vowel sign or diphthong sign through, or at the beginning or end of the stroke—

college,   accordance,   accordingly,   course,   court,   church,

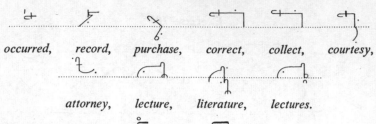

occurred,   record,   purchase,   correct,   collect,   courtesy,

attorney,   lecture,   literature,   lectures.

Distinctive Outlines: *regard*,   *regret*.

Exercise 71

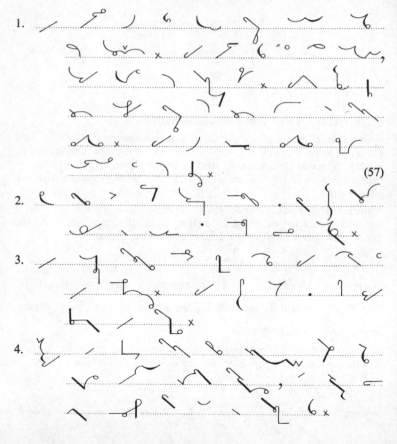

(57)

5.

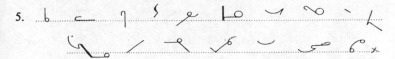

Exercise 72

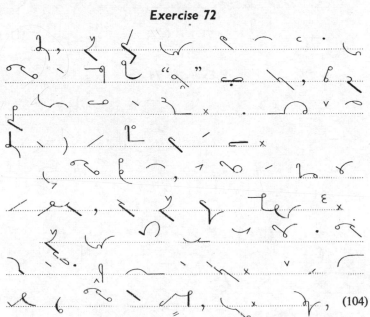

(104)

Exercise 73

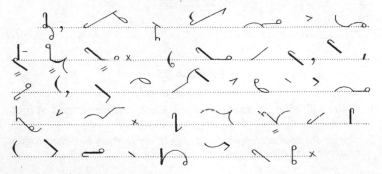

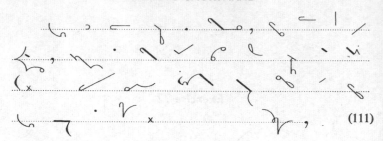

(111)

Exercise 74

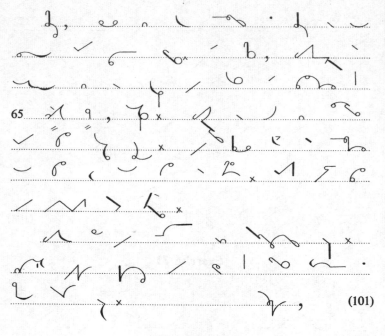

65

(101)

Exercise 75

(*Write in Shorthand*)

1. If-*you*-will bring *me a* supply *of*-samples *of-this* new breakfast food, *I*-will-try *to*-close-*the* deal *with-the* firm *myself*.

2. *During-the* course *of*-my lecture, *I-shall* try *to* show *how-the* progress *of* art *is* related *to-the* growth *of* industry.

3. *When I*-know *what-the* proposed water power scheme includes, *I-shall-be*-glad *to*-express my views.

4. *A* loud voice troubles *and* annoys us. Pleasant voices resemble sweet music.

5. Castles *in-the* air *are* fabrics *which* soon crumble, *but* dreamers *have* solved many *a* pressing problem.

6. Few *people are* able *themselves to* better-*the* labour *of-those* they blame.

Exercise 76
(*Write in Shorthand*)

Dear-Sirs, *Because-of-the* rapidly increasing cost *of* copper *and* steel, *we-are*-obliged *to* increase-*the* prices *of*-many *of-the* articles included *in* our catalogue. *We* extremely regret-*the* necessity *of* passing *on-the* higher charges *to-our* customers, *but* at-*the* present-time *this-is-the* only possible course *we-can* follow.

You-will-*be* notified *when* better terms *are* available *on-our* supplies, *and-we-are* thus enabled *to*-reduce-*the* prices. *Yours*-truly, (79)

42. Double Consonants—*Curves*

(*a*) A small initial hook, written on the inside of curves, forms a series of double consonant strokes, *fr*, *vr*, etc.—

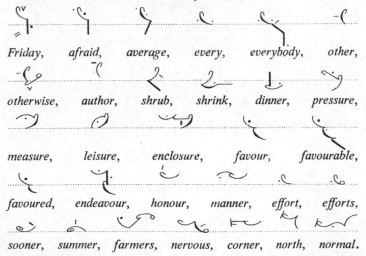

Friday, afraid, average, every, everybody, other,

otherwise, author, shrub, shrink, dinner, pressure,

measure, leisure, enclosure, favour, favourable,

favoured, endeavour, honour, manner, effort, efforts,

sooner, summer, farmers, nervous, corner, north, normal.

(b) A large initial hook, written on the inside of curves, forms the double consonants *fl*, *vl*, etc.—

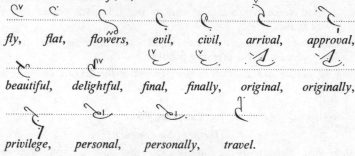

fly,   flat,   flowers,   evil,   civil,   arrival,   approval,

beautiful,   delightful,   final,   finally,   original,   originally,

privilege,   personal,   personally,   travel.

SHORT FORMS

⌒ nor (or *in our*), ⌒ near, ___ own, ___ owner, ⌒ more, remark or *remarked*, ⌒ remarkable, ⌒ Mr. or *mere*, ⌐ sure, ⌐ pleasure, ⌐ larger, ⌐ largely, ⌐ everything, ⌐ over, ⌐ however, ⌐ respectful-ly.

Exercise 77

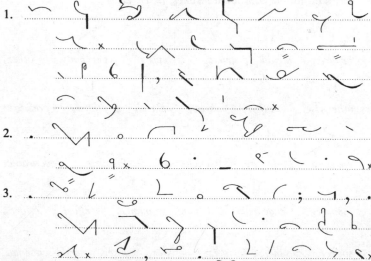

4.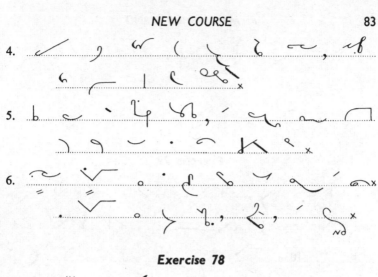

5.

6.

Exercise 78

1.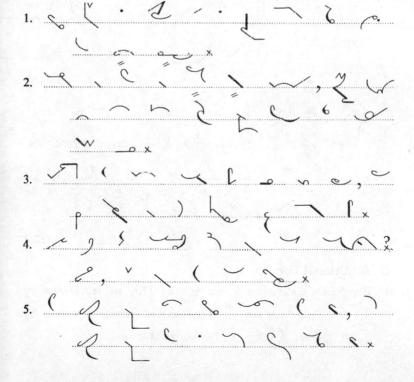

2.

3.

4.

5.

6.

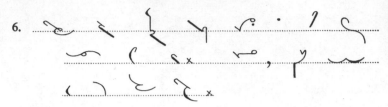

Exercise 79

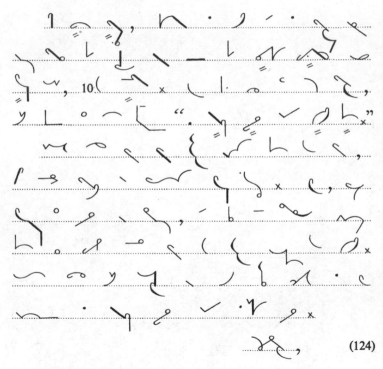

(124)

43. Additional Forms

(*a*) The double consonants *fr*, *vr*, *thr*, and *THr*, are represented by
   fr,   *vr*,   *thr*,   *THr* (reverse forms), as well as by
   fr,   *vr*,   *thr*,   *THr* (original forms).

When one of these double consonant strokes is the only stroke in the word, the reverse form is used *if the word does not begin with a vowel*—

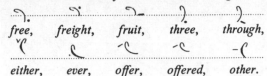

free,   *freight,*   *fruit,*   *three,*   *through,*

but   *either,*   *ever,*   *offer,*   *offered,*   *other.*

(*b*) When joined to another stroke, the forms are used which join most conveniently. Usually, the reverse forms are joined to strokes written towards the right—

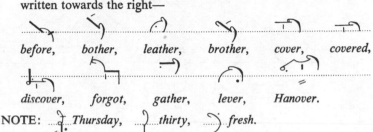

before,   *bother,*   *leather,*   *brother,*   *cover,*   *covered,*

discover,   *forgot,*   *gather,*   *lever,*   *Hanover.*

NOTE: *Thursday,*   *thirty,*   *fresh.*

(*c*) After *k, g, n,* or a straight upstroke, *fl* and *vl* are reversed—

rifle,   *reflect,*   *naval,*   *novel,*   *rival,*   *cavalry.*

44. The double consonant stroke *shl* is always written upward. The stroke *shr* is always written downward—

official,   *shelf,*   *partial,*   *specialize,*   *speciality,*   *essential,*

artificial,   *pressure,*   *Fisher.*

45. The heavy sign ⌣ is used to represent *ng-kr* or *ng-gr*—

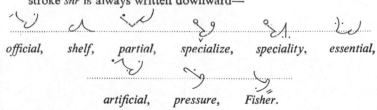

thinker,   *banker,*   *conquer,*   *finger,*   *stronger.*

SHORT FORMS

from,   *very,*   *they are,*   *their* or *there.*

Exercise 80

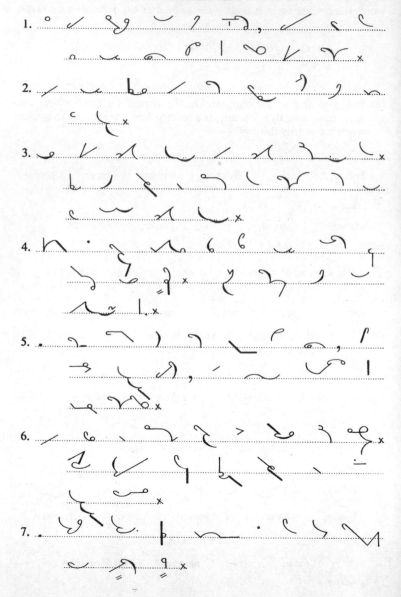

8.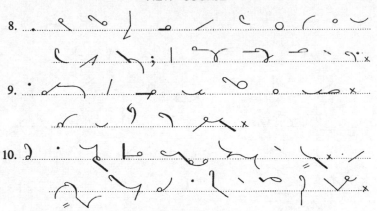

9.

10.

Exercise 81

1.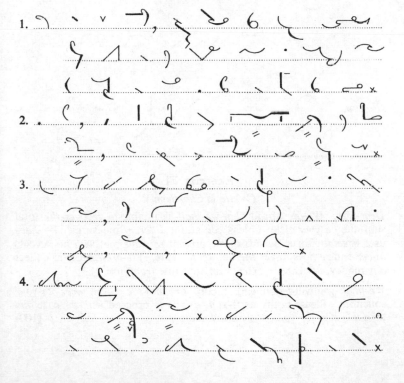

2.

3.

4.

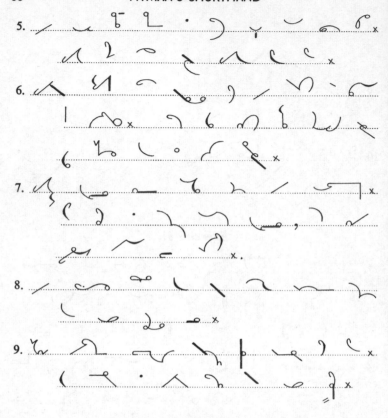

Exercise 82

(Write in Shorthand)

Dear-Sirs, *We-are* afraid *that-we-shall-be* unable-*to* recover-*the* total sum due *on-your* claim unless *you* adopt *different* measures. *We-have* used *special* efforts, *but* up *to-the* present *we-have* met *with* no success *in-our* endeavours *to-get-the* debtor *to* settle. *We-are*-unable-*to* collect *any* money, *nor can-we* extract *any* promise *from-him*.

We-think-you-will-*be*-obliged finally *to* pass-*the* claim *over to-your* solicitors. Please notify us if-*you wish*-us *to* proceed *with-the* case *and* take *this* step *for-you*. *Very*-truly-*yours*,　　　　　(100)

CHAPTER XII

46. *N* Hook

(*a*) A small final hook, written on the inside of curves, adds *n*—

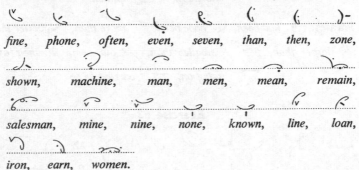

fine, phone, often, even, seven, than, then, zone,

shown, machine, man, men, mean, remain,

salesman, mine, nine, none, known, line, loan,

iron, earn, women.

(*b*) The *n* hook is written with a right (clockwise) motion at the end of all straight strokes—

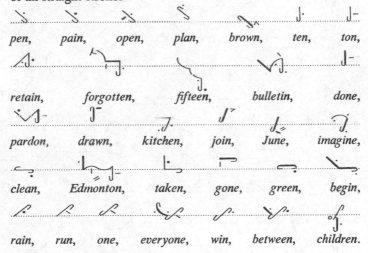

pen, pain, open, plan, brown, ten, ton,

retain, forgotten, fifteen, bulletin, done,

pardon, drawn, kitchen, join, June, imagine,

clean, Edmonton, taken, gone, green, begin,

rain, run, one, everyone, win, between, children.

Final *r*, when hooked, is usually written upward—

turn, return, learn, western, corn, pattern, Woburn.

SHORT FORMS

⟍ *been*,   ⟋ *general* or *generally*,   ⟨ *within*,   ⟨ *southern*,

⌣ *northern*,   ⌣ *opinion*.

Phrases: ⟋ *had been*,   ⟍ *have been*,   ⌢ *more than*,   *better than*,

⟋ *larger than*,   *smaller than*,   *our own*,   *their own*,

going on,   *carried on*.

Exercise 83

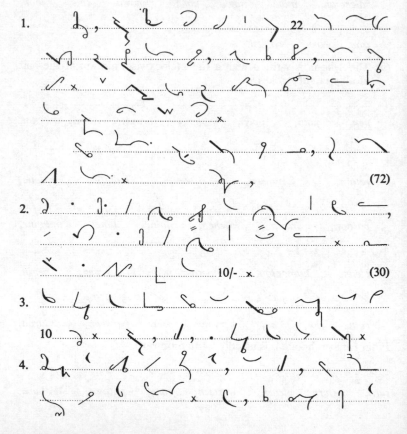

1.   ... 22 ... (72)

2.   ... 10/- ... (30)

3.   10 ...

4.   ...

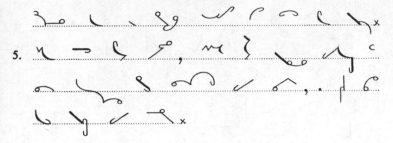

5.

Exercise 84

1.

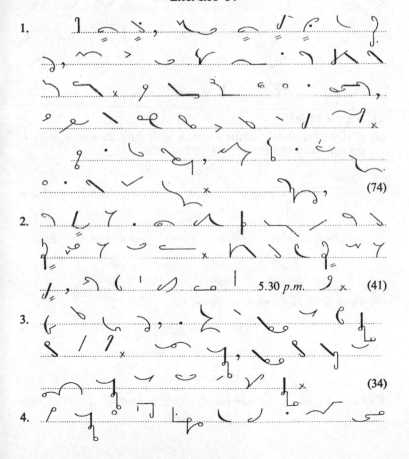

(74)

2.

5.30 p.m. (41)

3.

(34)

4.

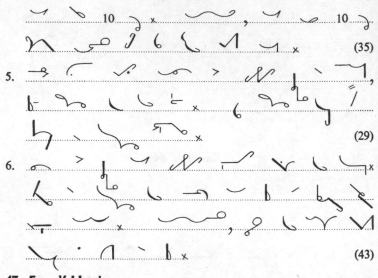

47. F or V Hook

(*a*) A small final hook, written with a left (anticlockwise) motion at the end of all straight strokes, adds *f* or *v*—

brief,   proof or *prove*,   approve,   above,   active,   relative,

attractive,   drive,   achieve,   gave,   rough,   serve,   deserve,

preserve,   reserve,   wife,   half.

(*b*) There is no *f* or *v* hook to curves.

SHORT FORMS

represent or *represented*,   *representative*,   *behalf*,   *advantage*.

Phrases: *out of*, *number of*, *instead of*, *which have*, *who have*.

Exercise 85

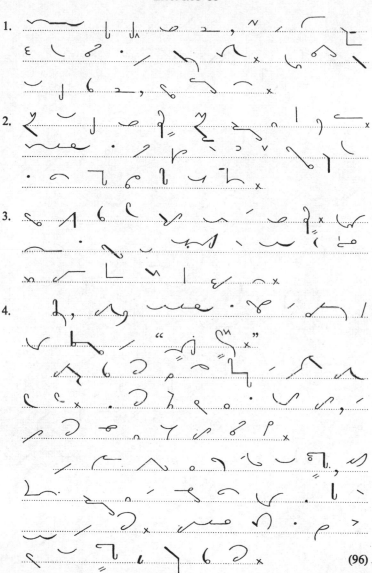

(96)

Exercise 86

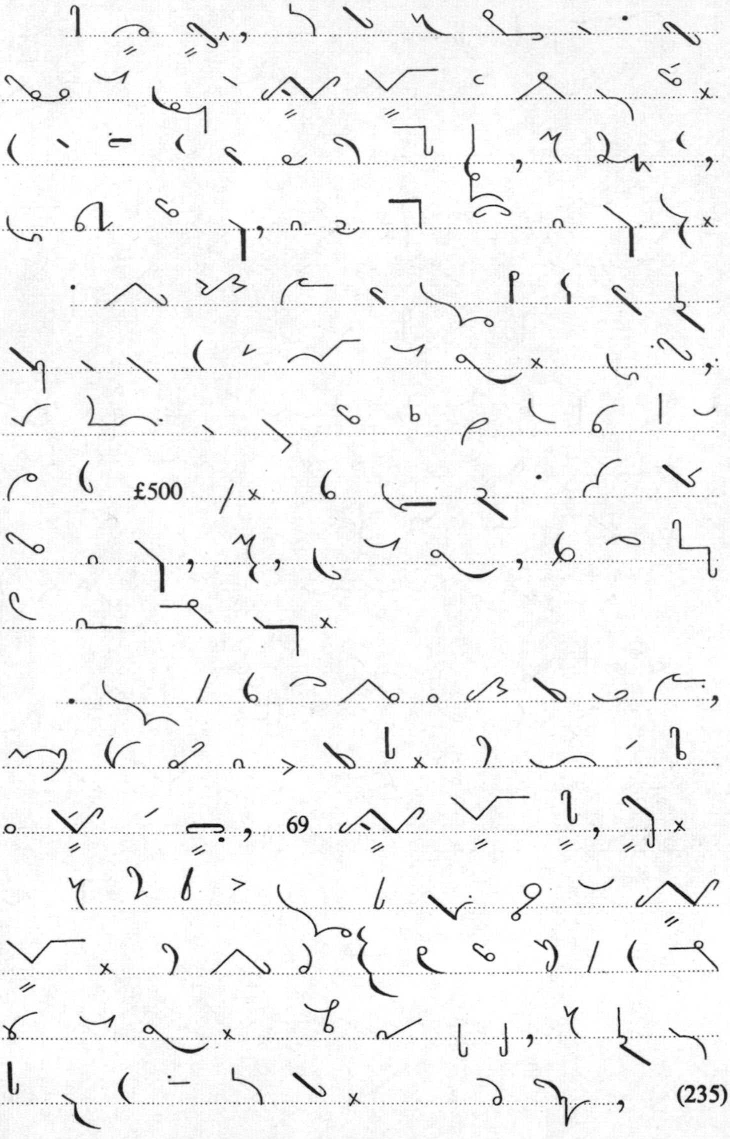

(235)

48. A finally hooked stroke is halved to indicate a following *t* or *d*—

(a) *find,   found,   event,   meant* or *mend,   demand,   mind,*

amount,   moment,   statement,   payment,   movement,   settlement,

shipment,   friend,   front,   department,   land,   around.

(b) *opened,   band,   print,   plant* or *planned,   spent* or *spend,   point,*

pound,   bound,   attend,   extent or *extend,   instant,   assistant,*

stand,   president,   kind,   count,   account,   discount,   second,

grand,   inclined,   went,   want,   turned,   current,   round,   returned.

(c) *approved,   gift,   served,   draft,   achieved,   deserved,*

reserved,   observed.

SHORT FORMS

gentleman,   gentlemen,   cannot,   told,   tried,   trade or *toward,   third.*

Phrases: *had not* or *do not,   did not.*

If it is necessary to indicate in your shorthand notes that a longhand abbreviation is to be used, write a fully vocalized outline for the abbreviation—

hadn't,   don't,   didn't,   doesn't,   haven't,   won't,   isn't,   couldn't,   can't.

NOTE: *can not* (separate words).

Exercise 87

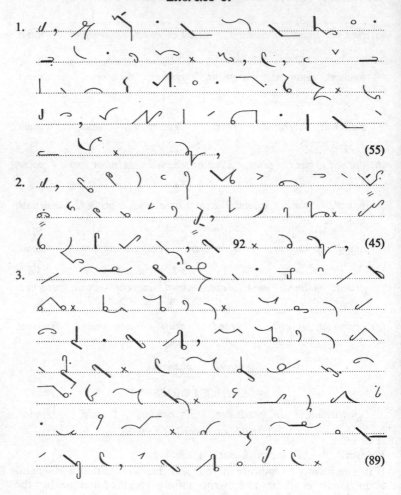

1. (55)

2. 92 (45)

3. (89)

Exercise 88

1.

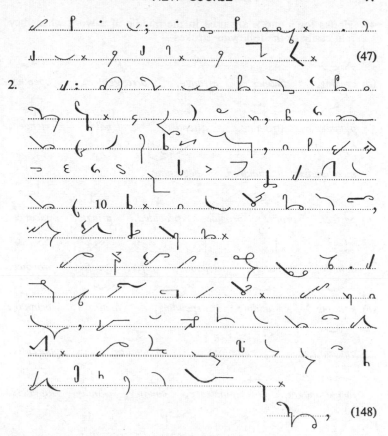

(47)

(148)

Exercise 89

(Write in Shorthand)

Gentlemen, Please *be* kind-enough *to* supply-*the* items on-*the* attached list *as*-soon-*as*-possible. At-*the* present moment *there-is an* active demand *for-them, and-we*-hope *that-we-can* count on having *them within* three days. If-*you* find *that-you-cannot* supply *them within that*-time, please-*inform*-us by return.

Please-note-*that-the* exact items specified *are to-be* supplied. If-*you-are* out-*of* stock *of any of-the* items, *do*-not supply *different* articles. *Anything that-is*-not exactly *as* specified will-*be* returned. *Yours*-truly,

(95)

49. Hooks for *v* and *n* are used in the middle of a word when they join easily to the following strokes—

(a) *evening,   finance,   arrange,   arrangement,   opening,*

planning,   training,   attended,   splendid,   extended,

merchandise,   hundred,   beginning.

(b) *perfect,   profit,   provide,   provided,   private,   advance,*

definite,   definitely,   telephone,   refer,   prefer,   province.

(c) *pointing,   standing,   spending,   finding,   printing,*

amounting,   mountain,   extending,   apparently,

memorandum,   correspondence,   country,   kindly,   kindness.

but note: *wanted,   printed,   meantime,   seconded,   accounted.*

Exercise 90

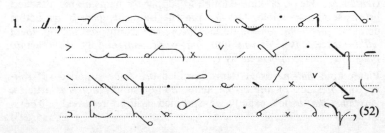

1.   (52)

2.

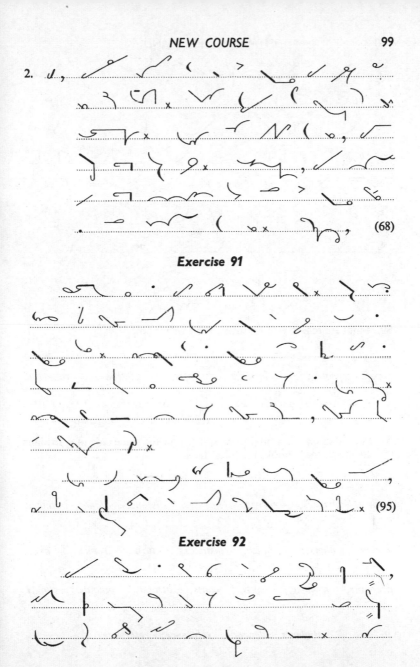

(68)

Exercise 91

(95)

Exercise 92

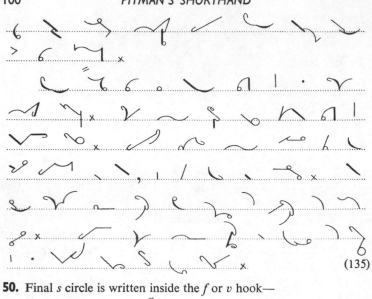

(135)

50. Final *s* circle is written inside the *f* or *v* hook—

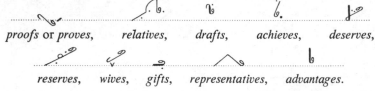

proofs or *proves,*   *relatives,*   *drafts,*   *achieves,*   *deserves,*

reserves,   *wives,*   *gifts,*   *representatives,*   *advantages.*

51. A final circle, or a final loop, written on the same side of a straight
stroke as the *n* hook, includes the *n*—

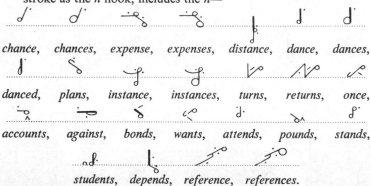

chance, chances, expense, expenses, distance, dance, dances,

danced, plans, instance, instances, turns, returns, once,

accounts, against, bonds, wants, attends, pounds, stands,

students, depends, reference, references.

52. A circle written inside an *n* hook attached to a full-length curve adds the final sound *z* only—

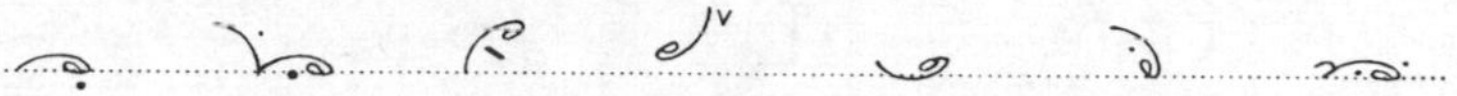

means, remains, loans, shines, opinions, earns, women's.

A circle written inside an *n* hook attached to a half-length curve adds the final sound *s* or *z*: *events, demands.*

53. After a curved stroke the light sound *-nce* is represented by stroke *n* and the final *s* circle—

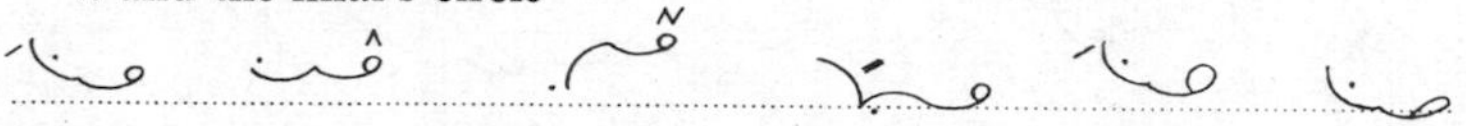

offence, announce, allowance, romance, offences, fenced,

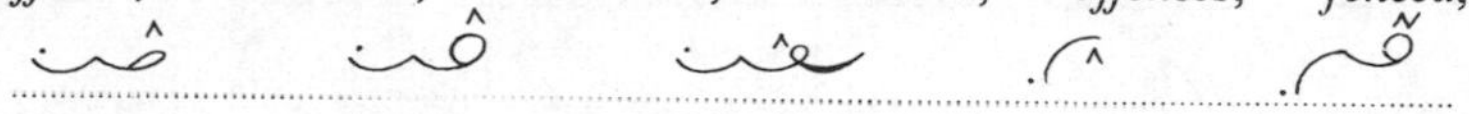

announced, announces, announcing, allow, allowances.

54. When a vowel follows *f*, *v*, or *n*, at the end of a word, it is necessary to write the stroke in order to be able to indicate the following vowel—

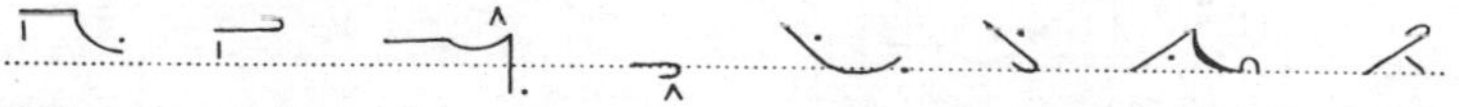

coffee, cough, county, count, penny, pen, review, rough.

SHORT FORMS

difficult, difficulty, balance, balanced,

responsible-ility, great, guard, gold.

Phrase: *at once.*

Exercise 93

1. 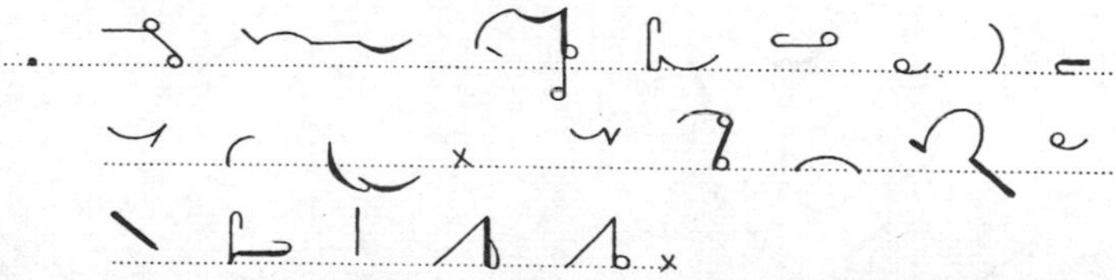

2. 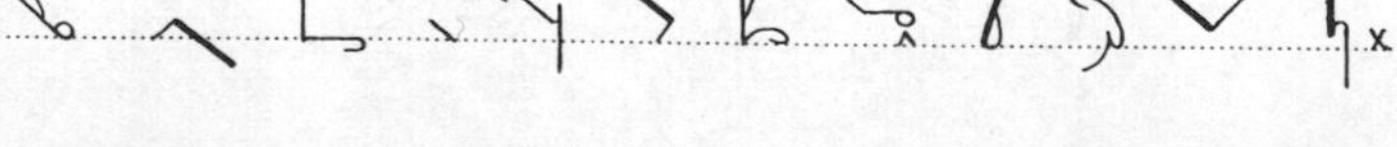

3.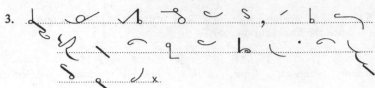

4.

5.

6.

7.

8.

Exercise 94

1.

2.

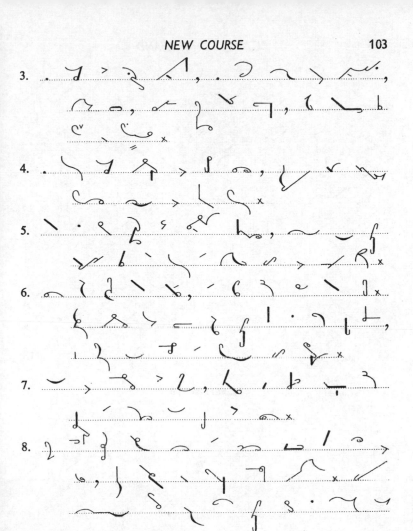

Exercise 95

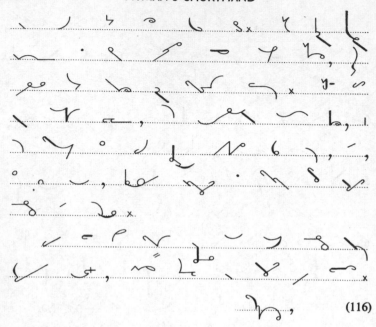

(116)

Exercise 96

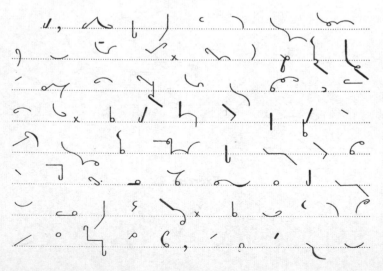

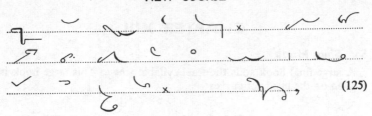

(125)

Exercise 97

(Write in Shorthand)

1. *This* firm gave us excellent references, so *we-think-we should* extend-*the* time *for*-payment *of-the balance* due *on-their*-account.

2. *The young*-man stands *a very*-good chance *of* obtaining-*the* post *of* assistant manager *of-the* bond department *owing to-the* splendid training hc-*has* received.

3. Please provide us *with a* memorandum *of all* merchandise *which-is subject to a special* allowance.

4. *The* rough draft serves *to* show *how-the* use *of-the* telephone *has-been* extended *during-the* last seven *years*.

5. *Several of-the* students *have-been* taken out-*of-the* second grade, *and-we* plan *to*-make other arrangements *for-those-who* remain.

6. *Your* statement *is* returned *because-the* amount *of-the* discount *that-you have* deducted *is*-not correct.

Exercise 98

(Write in Shorthand)

Gentlemen, We should-be ungrateful indeed if-*we*-did-not accept *your* kind hint. *As a* direct result *we-have* planned *a* series *of* trips *for our representatives which*-will bring *them* into closer touch *with our* customers *all-over-the* country. *Our* men *are* leaving at-once *with* samples *of-our* advance lines. They-will explain *to-you-the* reasons *for-the* apparent slackness *we-have* shown *during-the* past season. *It-has-been* one *of-much* stress *for*-us, *and-we-are*-inclined-*to-think* you-will make-*the* proper allowances *when-you* learn-*the* reason.

You-will-be-glad *to* know *that-the* new lines *to-be* shown *to-you have-been* favourably received *in-the* east. They-*are of* splendid value, *and are* sold at-prices *that give-us a very*-low margin *of*-profit. *Yours very*-truly,

(144)

CHAPTER XIII

55. -Shun Hook

A large final hook adds the final syllable *-shun*. This large hook is written on the inside of curves—

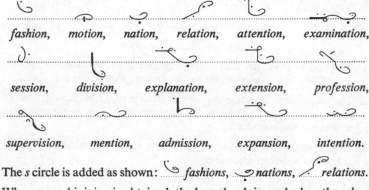

fashion,   motion,   nation,   relation,   attention,   examination,

session,   division,   explanation,   extension,   profession,

supervision,   mention,   admission,   expansion,   intention.

The *s* circle is added as shown: ⌣ *fashions*, ⌒ *nations*, ⌒ *relations*.

When a good joining is obtained, the large hook is used when the *-shun* syllable occurs in the middle of a word—

national,   professional,   intentional.

Exercise 99

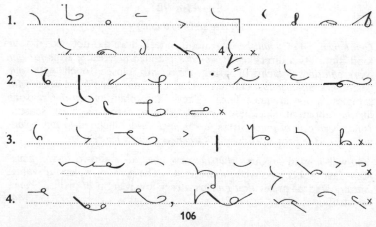

106

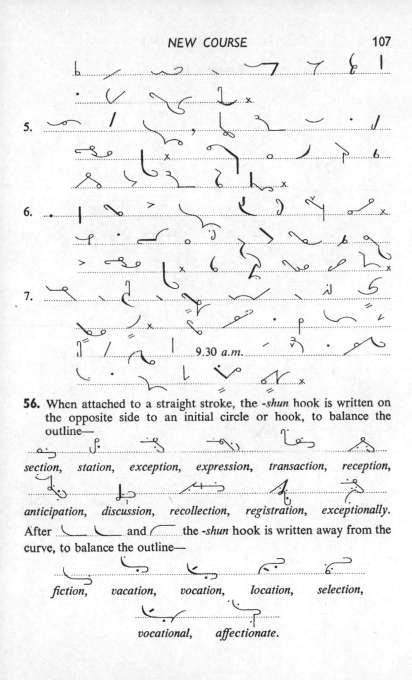

56. When attached to a straight stroke, the *-shun* hook is written on the opposite side to an initial circle or hook, to balance the outline—

section, station, exception, expression, transaction, reception,

anticipation, discussion, recollection, registration, exceptionally.

After ‿ ‿ and ⌒ the *-shun* hook is written away from the curve, to balance the outline—

fiction, vacation, vocation, location, selection,

vocational, affectionate.

Exercise 100

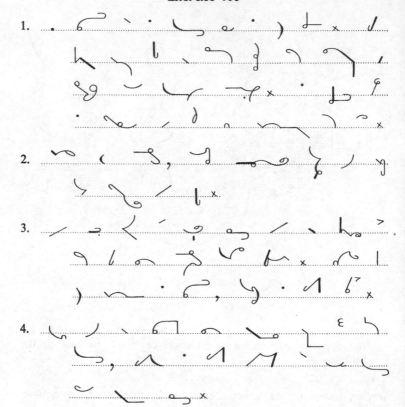

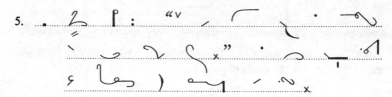

7.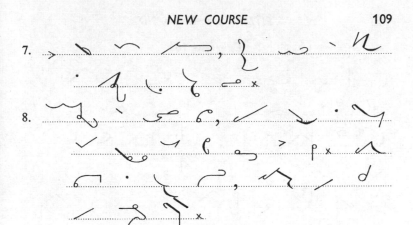

8.

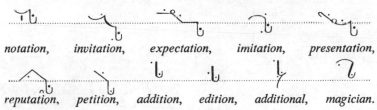

57. The -*shun* hook is written on the right side of simple *t*, *d*, or *j*—

notation,   invitation,   expectation,   imitation,   presentation,

reputation,   petition,   addition,   edition,   additional,   magician.

When added to other simple straight strokes, -*shun* is written on the side opposite to the last vowel—

action,   caution,   portion,   operation,   occasion,   education,

application,   distribution,   election,   direction,   attraction,

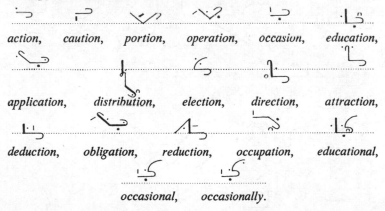

deduction,   obligation,   reduction,   occupation,   educational,

occasional,   occasionally.

Exercise 101

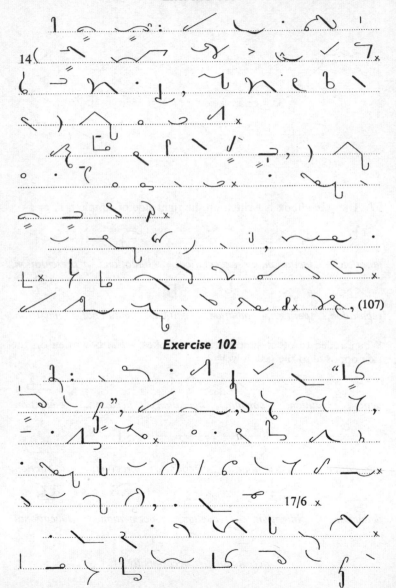

Exercise 102

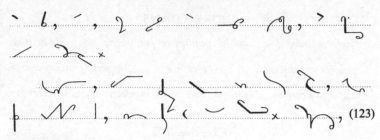

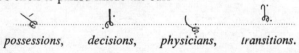

(123)

58. S-Shun

When *-shun* follows the *s* circle or the *ns* circle, it is represented by a small curl (a continuation of the circle). A third-place vowel between the *s* and *-shun* is placed outside the curl. Any other vowel is not indicated.

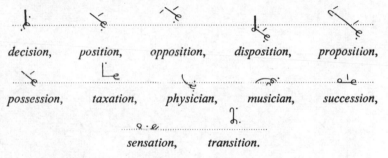

decision, position, opposition, disposition, proposition,

possession, taxation, physician, musician, succession,

sensation, transition.

A final *s* circle is placed inside the curl—

possessions, decisions, physicians, transitions.

59. In words ending in *-uation* or *-uition*, the stroke *sh* and *n* hook are generally used—

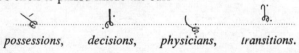

situation, tuition.

A stroke hooked for *-shun* is halved to indicate a final *t* or *d*—

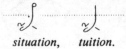

motioned, cautioned, fashioned.

SHORT FORMS

information,   *public, publish* or *published*,   *publication*,

object or *objected*,   *objection*,   *organize* or *organized*,

organization,   *satisfaction*,   *investigation*,   *yesterday*.

Exercise 103

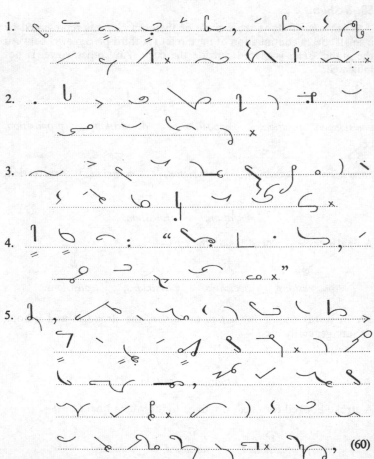

Exercise 104

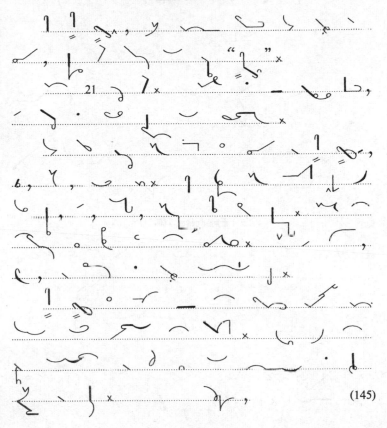

(145)

Exercise 105

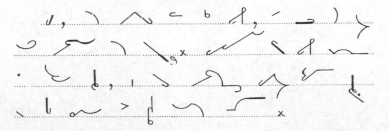

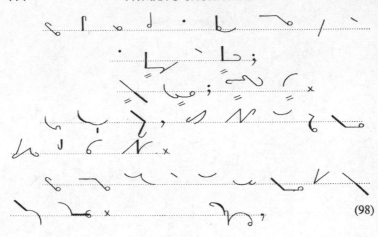

(98)

Exercise 106

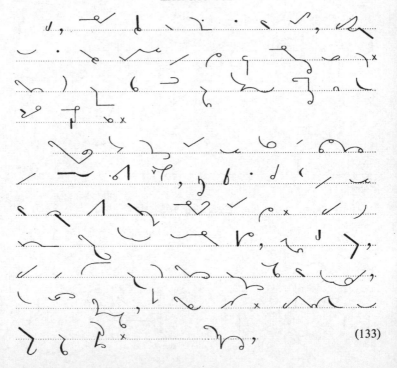

(133)

Exercise 107

(*Write in Shorthand*)

Gentlemen, We-think-we-are in a position *to* assist *you to-tell in what* direction *your* promotion work may best *be* extended. *As you-are-*no-doubt aware, *our organization has given* many *years of* attention *to* problems *of* distribution *of-*every *description, and-the information in-our-*possession *is very* reliable.

*We-believe-that-you would-*find *a* discussion *of-the* problem *with our* **Mr.** Jones *of-*value *to-you*. He-will-*be-*glad *to-*receive *an* invitation *from-you to-call. Very-*truly-*yours,* (87)

Exercise 108

(*Write in Shorthand*)

*Dear-*Sir, *With-the* small amount *of information in-our-*possession, *we-are-*unable-*to give-you a* definite decision *on-your* application *for a* loan. *You-*make no mention at-*all of any* provision *for* expansion at-*your* present factory, *nor do-you tell-*us *if-you have any* intention *of-*taking *over-the* operation *of more* machines.

However, we-believe-that-the proposition *is* certainly worth discussion, *although* action must, *of-*course, wait *till-you* supply us *with* additional *information* about *your* plans.

*We-*suggest *that-you call* at-*our* office sometime *during-the-next* few days, *to-*permit us *to-*go *over* every detail *of-the* situation *with-you.* *Yours-*truly, (114)

CHAPTER XIV

60. Compound Consonants

Besides the double consonants in the *pel* and *per* series, there are six compound consonants—

Letter	Sign	Name	As in
KW	⌐	*kwa*	quick, request
GW	⌐	*gwa*	Guelph, linguist
MP, MB	⌒	*emp* } *emb* }	camp, embody
LR	⌐	*ler*	filler, scholar
RR	⌐	*rer*	poorer, sharer
WH	⌐	*hwa*	where, whip

NOTE: *Ler* is used only where the downward *l* would be used; *rer* is used only where the downward *r* would be used.

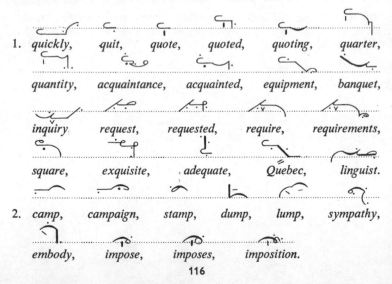

1. *quickly,   quit,   quote,   quoted,   quoting,   quarter,*

quantity,   acquaintance,   acquainted,   equipment,   banquet,

inquiry,   request,   requested,   require,   requirements,

square,   exquisite,   adequate,   Québec,   linguist.

2. *camp,   campaign,   stamp,   dump,   lump,   sympathy,*

embody,   impose,   imposes,   imposition.

116

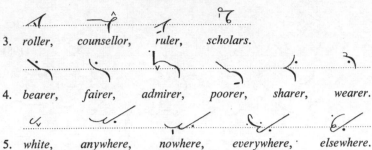

3. *roller, counsellor, ruler, scholars.*

4. *bearer, fairer, admirer, poorer, sharer, wearer.*

5. *white, anywhere, nowhere, everywhere, elsewhere.*

When *m* is immediately followed by *pr, br, pl,* or *bl,* the double consonant strokes ⟍ ⟍ ⟍ ⟍ are used—

impress, embrace, imply, emblem.

SHORT FORMS

whether, *important* or *importance,* *improve, improved* or *improvement,* *impossible,* *child,* *chaired,* *cheered,* *accord* or *according* (or *according to*), *cared,* *particular,* *opportunity.*

Phrases: *according to,* *according to the.*

Exercise 109

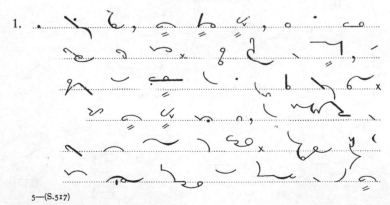

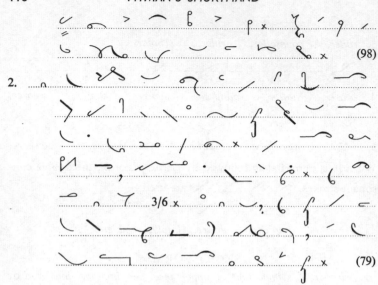

(98)

2.

(79)

Exercise 110

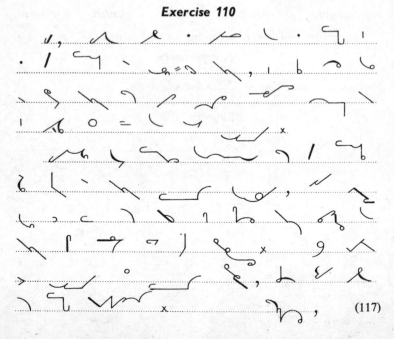

(117)

Exercise 111

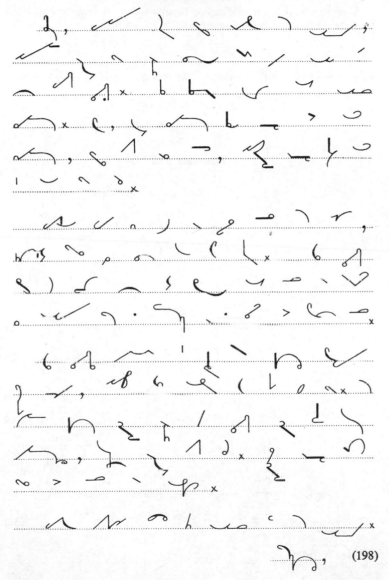

(198)

61. Wl and Whl

A small initial hook prefixes *w* to upward *l*. A large initial hook prefixes *wh* to upward *l*. These hooks are read first—

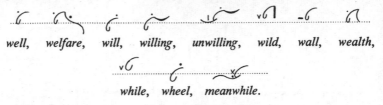

well, welfare, will, willing, unwilling, wild, wall, wealth,

while, wheel, meanwhile.

Exercise 112

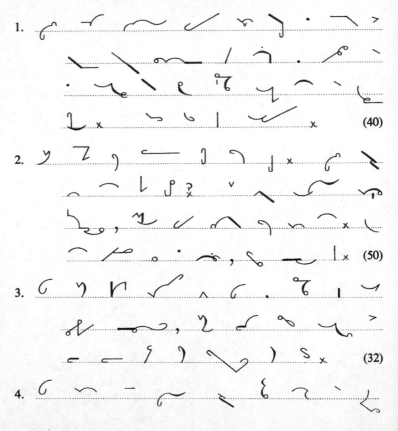

1. (40)

2. (50)

3. (32)

4.

(57)

62. Tick and Dot *H*

Generally the upward form of *h* is used when this stroke is joined to other consonants. When *h* is the only consonant, or when it is followed by *k* or *g*, the downward form is used—

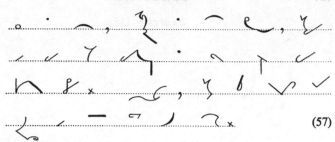

he,   hug,   hog,   hook,   high,   highway.

(*a*) The upward form is used for half-length *h* standing alone—

hate,   hot,   hat,   heat,   height.

(*b*) A small tick, written as shown, represents *h* before *m*, *l*, and downward *r*—

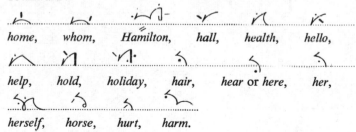

home,   whom,   Hamilton,   hall,   health,   hello,

help,   hold,   holiday,   hair,   hear or here,   her,

herself,   horse,   hurt,   harm.

(*c*) Where it would be awkward to write the stroke *h* in the middle of a word, *h* is represented by a light dot placed alongside the vowel sound, in words such as—

perhaps,   neighbourhood,   likelihood,   household,   Manhattan.

Exercise 113

1. [shorthand outlines]

2. [shorthand outlines]

3. [shorthand outlines]

4. [shorthand outlines]

5. [shorthand outlines]

(45)

6. [shorthand outlines]

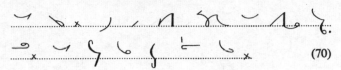

(70)

63. Omission of Consonants

(a) Where a medial *t* is only lightly sounded after circle *s*, it may sometimes be omitted, as in—

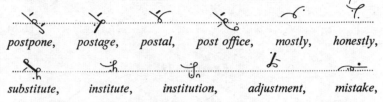

postpone,   postage,   postal,   post office,   mostly,   honestly,

substitute,   institute,   institution,   adjustment,   mistake,

mistaken,   investigate.

(b) Other lightly sounded consonants may sometimes be omitted, as in—

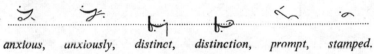

anxious,   unxiously,   distinct,   distinction,   prompt,   stamped.

Exercise 114

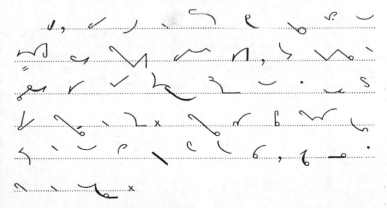

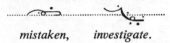

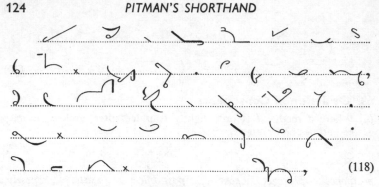

(118)

Exercise 115

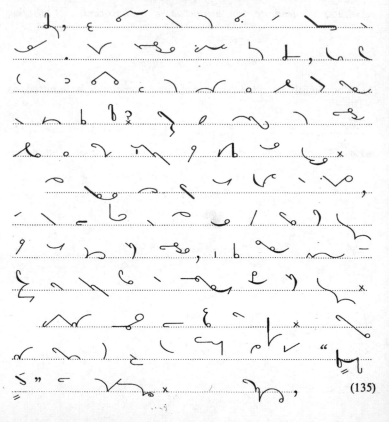

(135)

Exercise 116

(*Write in Shorthand*)

1. *Gentlemen, We-are* anxious *to*-receive-*the* pens *which according-to your* invoice *of* 14th *November* were *sent* by post five days ago. *We*-presume *that-the* parcel *was sent* by registered post.

   In-answer *to-our* inquiry, *the* post-office here says *that-the* package *has*-not-yet-*been* received. *Do-you think that-there-has-been a* mistake *in* addressing *it*? *Yours very*-truly,   (66)

2. *Gentlemen, We-are*-sorry *to*-learn *that-the* package *we-sent to-you* by registered post *on* 14th *November has*-not-*been* received. Promptly upon receipt *of-your* note *we-sent a* duplicate. *It-is*-possible, *of*-course, *that-the* label *was* incorrectly addressed, *but-we-do*-not-*think that-there-is any* likelihood *that-this-is-the* case. *We-are* asking-*the* postal authorities *to* institute *a* search *for-the* lost parcel, *and*-no-doubt they-will-*be*-able-*to* find *it*.

   Meanwhile, if-*the* original package *is delivered to-you*, will-*you*-kindly return *it* to-us. *The* cost *of* postage will-*be-sent to-you*, or *you-can* make *an* adjustment *in-your*-account *when-you* post *your* cheque. *Very*-truly-*yours*,   (125)

CHAPTER XV

64. Halving

There are a few additional applications of the halving principle.

(a) The strokes *m* and *n* are halved and thickened to indicate a following *d*—

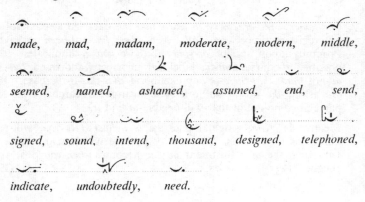

made, mad, madam, moderate, modern, middle,

seemed, named, ashamed, assumed, end, send,

signed, sound, intend, thousand, designed, telephoned,

indicate, undoubtedly, need.

(b) Downward *l* and downward *r* are halved and thickened to indicate a following *d*—

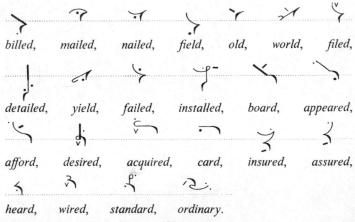

billed, mailed, nailed, field, old, world, filed,

detailed, yield, failed, installed, board, appeared,

afford, desired, acquired, card, insured, assured,

heard, wired, standard, ordinary.

Exercise 117

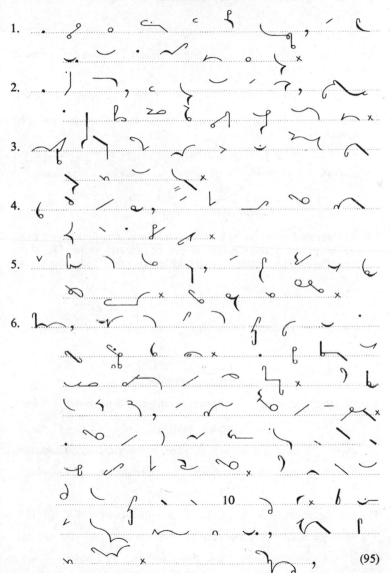

(95)

65. Final *lt* is expressed by ⌒, and final *rt* is generally expressed by ⟋ —

belt,   felt,   built,   fault,   bolts,   start,   support,   smart,

sort,   skirt,   part,   ports,   sport,   report,   export,   import.

66. When a vowel comes between *l-d* or *r-d*, the full strokes must be written—

carried,   delayed,   followed,   married,   valued,

borrowed,   worried.

67. As indicated in paragraph 35 (*b*), strokes of unequal length must not be joined if their length would not clearly show. To show the difference in length, disjoin half-length *t* or *d* following stroke *t* or *d*—

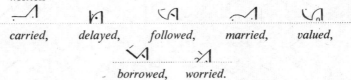

attitude,   credited,   treated,   dictated,   straightened,

illustrated,   post-dated.

Special use of disjoining: promptness, indebtedness, outfit.

SHORT FORMS

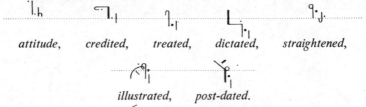

short, hand, under, yard, word, immediate, school, schooled, spirit, certificate, knowledge, acknowledge.

The halving principle is used to form such phrases as *if it*, *if it is*, *in which it is*, *I am not*, *you are not*, *you will not*, *you were not*, *this would be*, *I would*.

Exercise 118

1.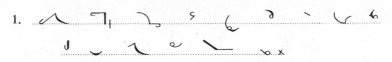

2.

3.

4.

5.

6.

7.

8.

Exercise 119

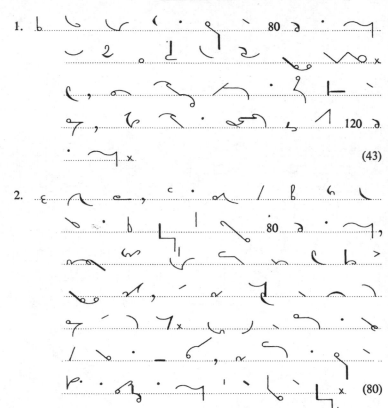

1. [shorthand outlines] 80 [shorthand outlines] (43)

2. [shorthand outlines] 80 [shorthand outlines] (80)

Exercise 120

1. [shorthand outlines] (43)

2.

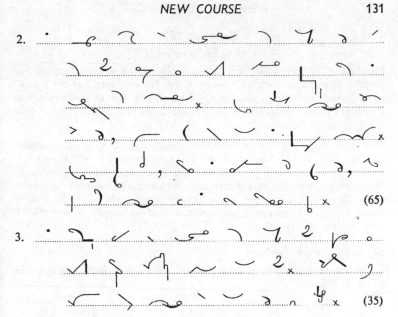

(65)

3.

(35)

Exercise 121

(110)

Exercise 122

(Write in Shorthand)

Gentlemen, Please-*inform*-us *immediately* *when-we*-may *expect-the* lighting fixtures *we* ordered *from-you* on 7th October, *for-the* apartment house *we-are*-now *building.* *According-to* our *under*standing at *that*-time, *you*-were *to-deliver them towards-the* end *of-the*-month, *but-you have* failed *to do*-so.

*It-is under*stood, *of*-course, *that-the* delay may not *be* intentional *on-your* part, *but-we-have* received no *word from-you.* Please-*do*-not hesitate *to inform*-us if-*you-are*-not able-*to*-make *immediate delivery.* *We-think-you*-will-not mis*under*stand *our* attitude *when-we* say *that* if-*you-cannot deliver-them immediately we-shall-have to*-get *them* elsewhere. Work *is*-now *be*ing delayed, *and-we* simply *cannot* afford *to*-wait. *Very*-truly-*yours,*   (131)

68. Doubling Principle

Curved strokes are doubled in length to indicate a following syllable *tr, dr,* or *THr*—

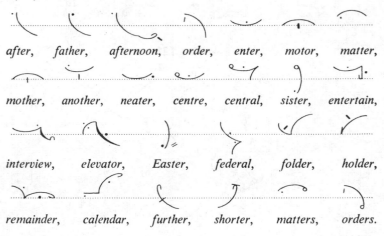

after,   father,   afternoon,   order,   enter,   motor,   matter,

mother,   another,   neater,   centre,   central,   sister,   entertain,

interview,   elevator,   Easter,   federal,   folder,   holder,

remainder,   calendar,   further,   shorter,   matters,   orders.

Stroke *l* standing alone, or with only a final *s* circle, is doubled to add *tr* only—

letter,   letters,   later,   latter,   alter, but *leader,*   older,   leather.

Exercise 123

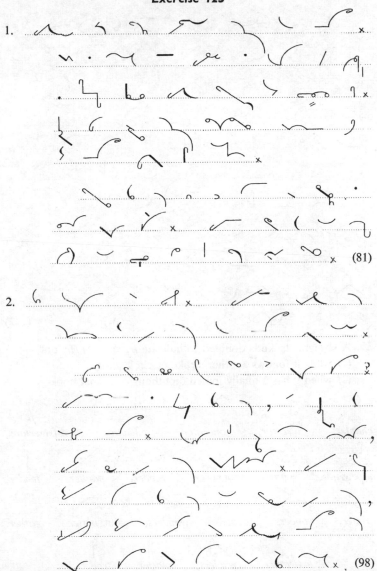

1. ... (81)

2. ... (98)

Exercise 124

(132)

69. A straight stroke is doubled to indicate *tr*, *dr*, or *THr*, only—
   (1) when it follows another stroke or circle *s*, or
   (2) when it has a finally joined diphthong or a final hook—

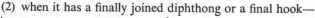

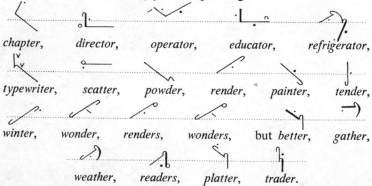

chapter,   director,   operator,   educator,   refrigerator,

typewriter,   scatter,   powder,   render,   painter,   tender,

winter,   wonder,   renders,   wonders,   but *better*,   gather,

weather,   readers,   platter,   trader.

70. In a few common words the syllable *-ture* is represented by the doubling principle—

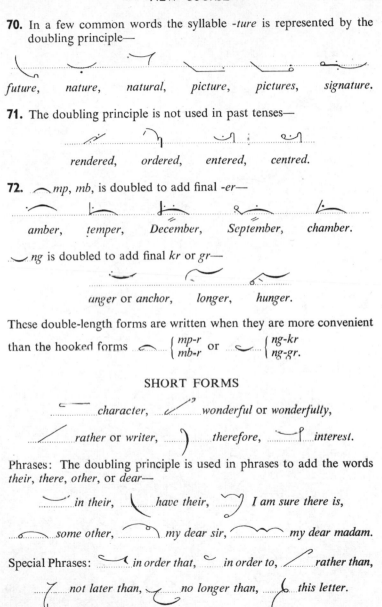

future,   nature,   natural,   picture,   pictures,   signature.

71. The doubling principle is not used in past tenses—

rendered,   ordered,   entered,   centred.

72. *mp, mb*, is doubled to add final *-er*—

amber,   temper,   December,   September,   chamber.

ng is doubled to add final *kr* or *gr*—

anger or anchor,   longer,   hunger.

These double-length forms are written when they are more convenient than the hooked forms ⁓ { *mp-r* / *mb-r* } or ⁓ { *ng-kr* / *ng-gr*. }

SHORT FORMS

character,   wonderful or wonderfully,

rather or writer,   therefore,   interest.

Phrases: The doubling principle is used in phrases to add the words *their, there, other,* or *dear*—

in their,   have their,   I am sure there is,

some other,   my dear sir,   my dear madam.

Special Phrases: in order that,   in order to,   rather than,

not later than,   no longer than,   this letter.

Exercise 125

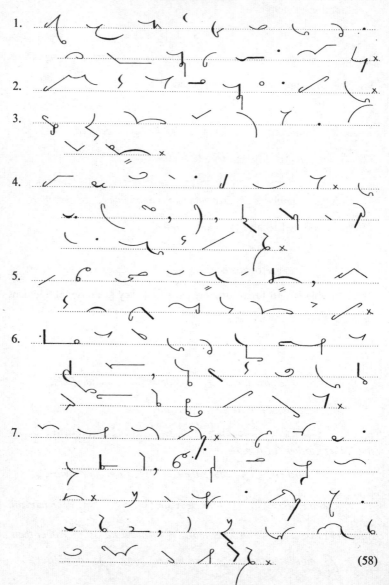

8.

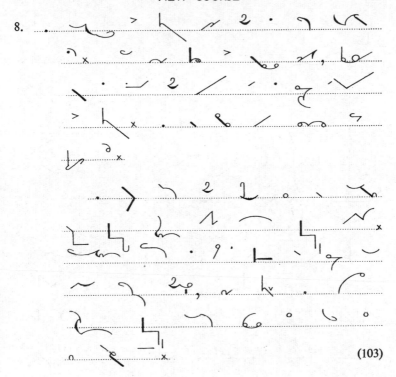

(103)

Exercise 126

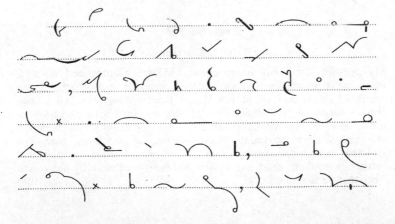

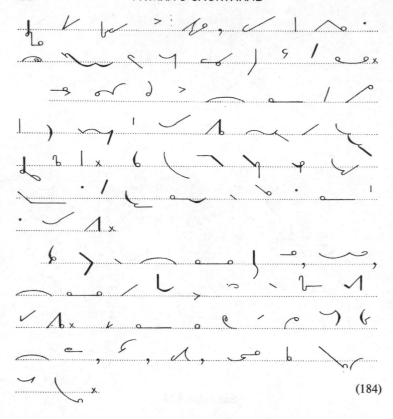

(184)

Exercise 127

(*Write in Shorthand*)

My-*dear*-Sir, *On behalf of-our*-clients, Messrs. Cantor *and* Walters, *who-have* requested us *to-represent their interests in-the*-matter *of-the* leasehold *on-the building* at 129 Wharf Street, *we-wish to inform-you that-we-have-their* permission *to* obtain *a* court order, *under-the* terms *of-which you*-will-not-*be*-able-*to* alter *the* front *of-the building.* *We-think-there-is* no-doubt *that-the*-terms *of-the* lease *have-been* violated, *and in-our-opinion it*-will-*be to-your* interest *to* stop *any* further operations until *a* decision *has-been* rendered by-*the* court. *Very*-truly-*yours,* (108)

CHAPTER XVI

73. Prefixes

(*a*) The prefix *con-*, or *com-*, is expressed by a dot, written first at the beginning of an outline, as shown. In words beginning with the *con-* or *com-* dot, the first vowel after the prefix determines the position of the outline—

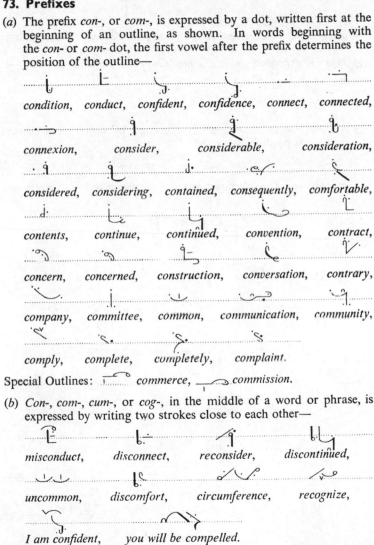

condition, conduct, confident, confidence, connect, connected,

connexion, consider, considerable, consideration,

considered, considering, contained, consequently, comfortable,

contents, continue, continued, convention, contract,

concern, concerned, construction, conversation, contrary,

company, committee, common, communication, community,

comply, complete, completely, complaint.

Special Outlines: ⎯ commerce, ⎯ commission.

(*b*) *Con-*, *com-*, *cum-*, or *cog-*, in the middle of a word or phrase, is expressed by writing two strokes close to each other—

misconduct, disconnect, reconsider, discontinued,

uncommon, discomfort, circumference, recognize,

I am confident, you will be compelled.

139

74. (a) *Accom-* or *accommo-* is expressed by _____ *k*, either joined or disjoined (always in the first position)—

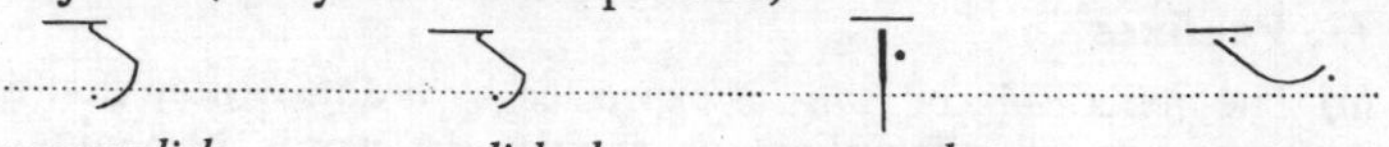

accomplish,   accomplished,   accommodate,   accompany.

(b) *Intro-* is expressed by _____ *ntr* (always in the third position)—

introduce,   introduced.

(c) *Magna-, magni-,* or *magne-* is expressed by disjoined *m* (always in the first position)—

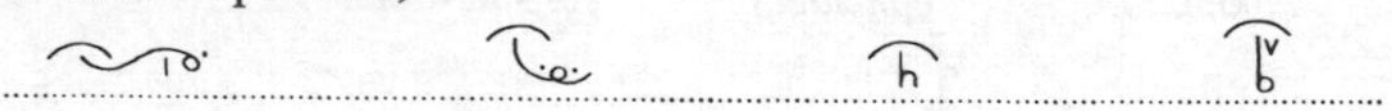

magnanimous,   magnificent,   magnitude,   magnetize.

Exercise 128

1.

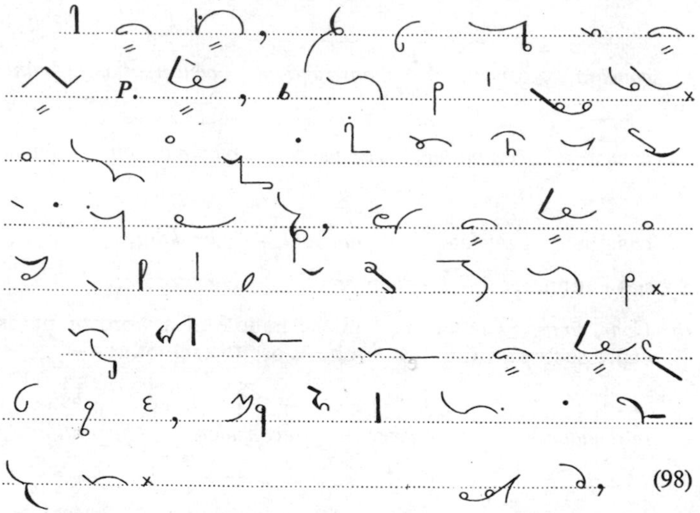

(98)

2.   14

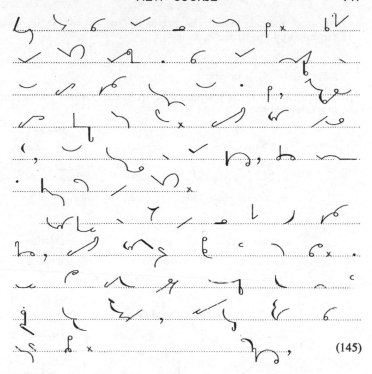

(145)

75. (a) *Self-* is expressed by a disjoined *s* circle, and *self-con-* is represented by writing the *s* circle in the place of the *con-* dot—

self-defence, self-esteem, self-satisfied, self-contained, self-control.

(b) *Trans-* may be contracted in most words by omitting the *n*—

transfer,   transportation,   translate,   transcribe.

(c) *In-* before str ⌐ skr ↗ h (upward) is expressed by a small hook, written in the same direction as the circle—

instruct,   instructed,   instrument,   inscriber,   inhabit.

(d) *Negative Words.* When the prefix *in-* means *not*, it is always expressed by the stroke *n*, as in—

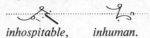

inhospitable, *inhuman.*

Other negative words are distinguished from the positive by repeating the first consonant—

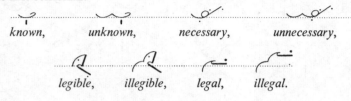

known, *unknown,* *necessary,* *unnecessary,*

legible, *illegible,* *legal,* *illegal.*

SHORT FORMS

commercial-ly, *inscribe-d,* *inscription,*
instructive, *instruction,* *circumstance,*
signify-ied-icant, *significance.*

Exercise 129

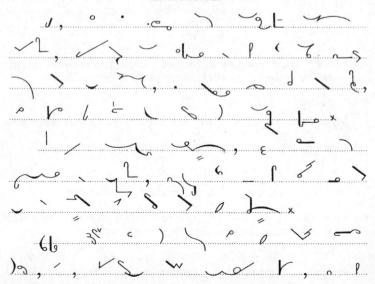

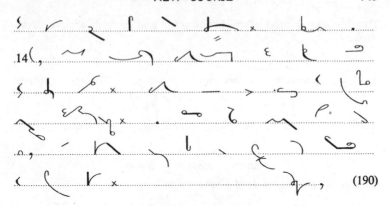

(190)

Exercise 130
(Write in Shorthand)

Gentlemen, We-received *your* communication *of-the* 14th, *in-which-you* complain *of-the* delay *in-the* completion *of-your* contract. *That-we-have* failed *to* accomplish *what we*-promised *we*-must admit, *and-we very*-much regret *our* failure.

We-are confident, *however, that-the* contract *could-have-been* completed *as* agreed upon *but for-the* recent trouble *with-the Commercial* Transport Committee, *which-was immediately responsible for-the* delay. *Their* decision interfered considerably *with our* business, *and-when-we* state *that* only thirty *of-our* transport men *have* continued at work, *we-think-you*-will recognize *how difficult it-has-been to* satisfy *our* customers.

It-is-unnecessary *for*-us *to* add *that-we should* regret-*the* transfer *of-your* business, considering-*the* long connexion between us, *and-the* cause *of-the* present interruption. *Very*-truly-*yours*,   (139)

76. Suffixes and Word-endings

Where it would be awkward to write ⌣ *ng* at the end of a word, the suffix -*ing* is represented by a light dot—

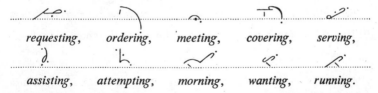

requesting,   ordering,   meeting,   covering,   serving,

assisting,   attempting,   morning,   wanting,   running.

The dot -*ing* is used after downward *r* and a light straight downstroke—

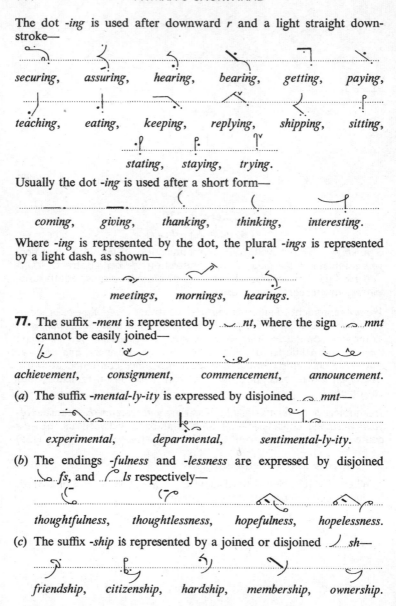

securing,   assuring,   hearing,   bearing,   getting,   paying,

teaching,   eating,   keeping,   replying,   shipping,   sitting,

stating,   staying,   trying.

Usually the dot -*ing* is used after a short form—

coming,   giving,   thanking,   thinking,   interesting.

Where -*ing* is represented by the dot, the plural -*ings* is represented by a light dash, as shown—

meetings,   mornings,   hearings.

77. The suffix -*ment* is represented by ⌣ *nt*, where the sign ⌒ *mnt* cannot be easily joined—

achievement,   consignment,   commencement,   announcement.

(*a*) The suffix -*mental-ly-ity* is expressed by disjoined ⌒ *mnt*—

experimental,   departmental,   sentimental-ly-ity.

(*b*) The endings -*fulness* and -*lessness* are expressed by disjoined ⌣ *fs*, and ⌒ *ls* respectively—

thoughtfulness,   thoughtlessness,   hopefulness,   hopelessness.

(*c*) The suffix -*ship* is represented by a joined or disjoined ⟋ *sh*—

friendship,   citizenship,   hardship,   membership,   ownership.

(d) -*Lity* or -*rity*, preceded by any vowel, is expressed by disjoining the preceding stroke—

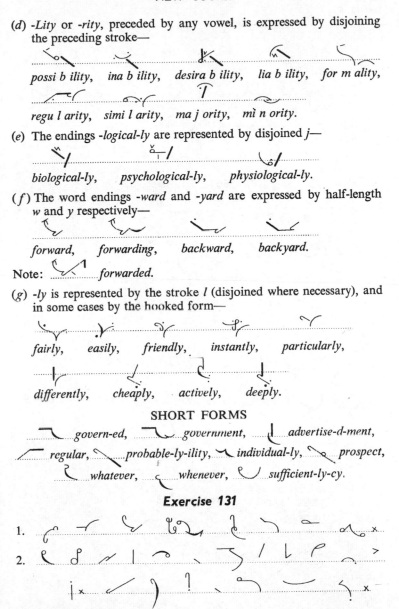

possi b ility,   ina b ility,   desira b ility,   lia b ility,   for m ality,

regu l arity,   simi l arity,   ma j ority,   mì n ority.

(e) The endings -*logical-ly* are represented by disjoined *j*—

biological-ly,   psychological-ly,   physiological-ly.

(f) The word endings -*ward* and -*yard* are expressed by half-length *w* and *y* respectively—

forward,   forwarding,   backward,   backyard.

Note: forwarded.

(g) -*ly* is represented by the stroke *l* (disjoined where necessary), and in some cases by the hooked form—

fairly,   easily,   friendly,   instantly,   particularly,

differently,   cheaply,   actively,   deeply.

SHORT FORMS

govern-ed,   government,   advertise-d-ment,   regular,   probable-ly-ility,   individual-ly,   prospect,   whatever,   whenever,   sufficient-ly-cy.

Exercise 131

1.

2.

3.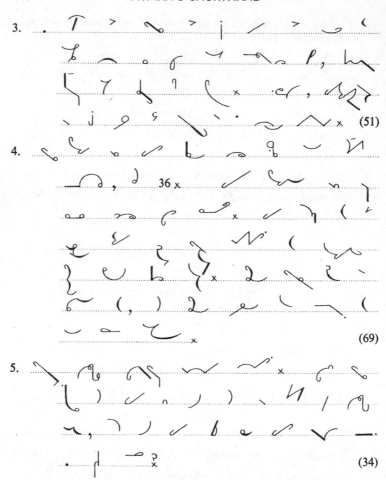

(51)

4.

(69)

5.

(34)

Exercise 132

1.

2.

3.

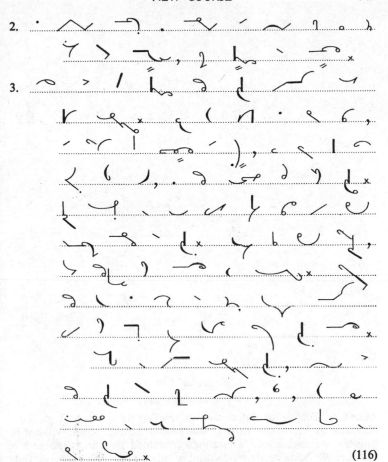

(116)

Exercise 133

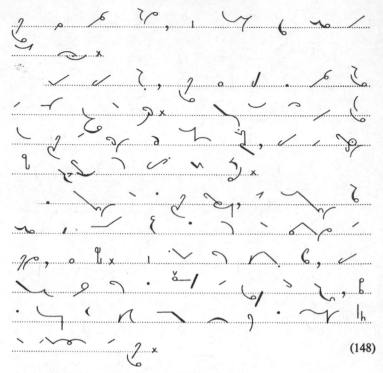

(148)

Exercise 134

(Write in Shorthand)

Dear-Sir, *Your*-letter dated *the* 4th reached us *this* morning. *Your instructions have-been* noted, *but-we-are* afraid *that-it*-will-not-*be* possible *to*-make *all-the* alterations contained *in-your* memorandum *and-have-the* book ready by-*the* end *of-this* month. *However*, we fully recognize-*the* desirability *of-having-the publication* completed at *an* early date, *and-we-are* requesting *our* printer *to* hasten-*the* setting *and* printing *as-much-as*-possible.

The inscription will-*be*-placed after-*the* title page, *as you* desire. Proofs *of-the* last chapters will-*be* forwarded *to-you within a* few days.

Announcements will-*be published in next* Saturday's papers *to-the* effect *that a* new novel by *a* prominent *writer* will *shortly* appear. Please *tell*-us if-*you would rather have*-us use *your* name *in-the* announcement. *Very*-truly-*yours*, (142)

CHAPTER XVII

78. Diphones

Two consecutive vowels, pronounced in two separate syllables, are represented by the angular signs ⌐ ⌐ These signs are called *Diphones*.

The first ⌐ represents a dot vowel followed by any other vowel, and the second ⌐ represents a dash vowel followed by any other vowel. The signs are written in the place of the first vowel of the combination.

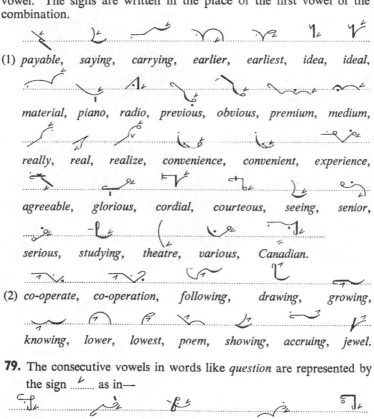

(1) *payable, saying, carrying, earlier, earliest, idea, ideal,*

material, piano, radio, previous, obvious, premium, medium,

really, real, realize, convenience, convenient, experience,

agreeable, glorious, cordial, courteous, seeing, senior,

serious, studying, theatre, various, Canadian.

(2) *co-operate, co-operation, following, drawing, growing,*

knowing, lower, lowest, poem, showing, accruing, jewel.

79.
The consecutive vowels in words like *question* are represented by the sign ⌐ as in—

question, union, suggestion, million, guardian.

80. Medial W

There is a small group of words in which *w* combined with a vowel in the middle of a word is represented by a small semicircle to give an easier or shorter outline. A left semicircle represents *w* followed by a dot vowel, and a right semicircle represents *w* followed by a dash vowel. The semicircles are written in the place of the vowel with which the *w* is combined—

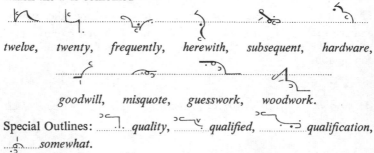

twelve, twenty, frequently, herewith, subsequent, hardware,

goodwill, misquote, guesswork, woodwork.

Special Outlines: _____ quality, _____ qualified, _____ qualification,

_____ somewhat.

81. Upward SH

The stroke ⟋ *sh* is written upward in certain cases to obtain a better outline—

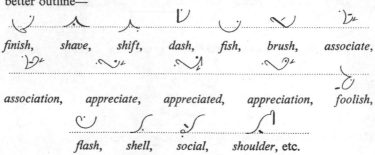

finish, shave, shift, dash, fish, brush, associate,

association, appreciate, appreciated, appreciation, foolish,

flash, shell, social, shoulder, etc.

82. Stroke R

To keep the outline close to the line of writing, the upward *r* is generally used where *r* follows two downstrokes. For the same reason, downward *r* is used finally after two straight upstrokes—

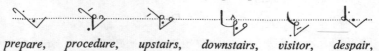

prepare, procedure, upstairs, downstairs, visitor, despair,

disappear,   treasurer,   furniture,   Shakespeare,   rarer.

83. Stroke S

The stroke *s* is written (*a*) in words like ⌣ *science,* ⌣ *scientific,* ⌣ *sighing,* ⌣ *Siam,* where a triphone immediately follows initial *s,* and (*b*) in words like ⌣ *continuous,* ⌣ *fatuous,* ⌣ *strenuous,* ⌣ *pious,* where the final syllable *-ous* is immediately preceded by a diphthong.

SHORT FORMS

⌣ *danger,* ⌣ *financial-ly,* ⌣ *mortgage-d,* ⌣ *neglect-ed,* ⌣ *practic(s)e-d,* ⌣ *university,* ⌣ *English,* ⌣ *exchange-d,* ⌣ *familiar-ity,* ⌣ *telegram.*

Exercise 135

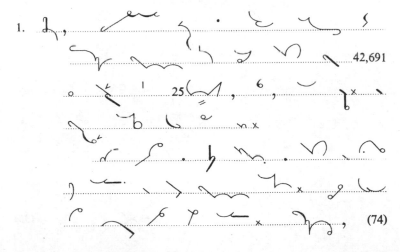

1.

42,691

25

6

(74)

2.

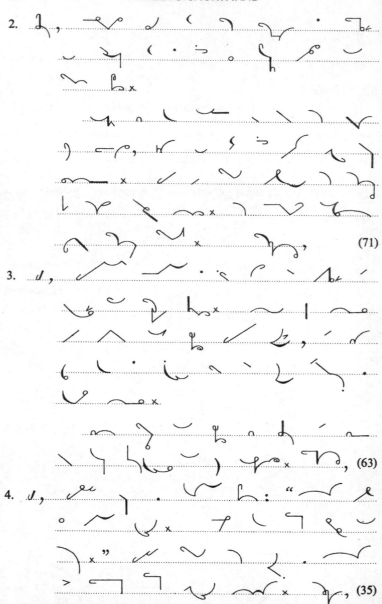

(71)

3.

(63)

4.

(35)

5.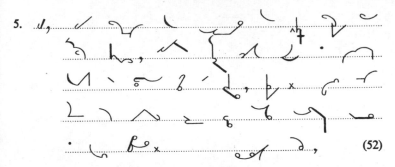

(52)

Exercise 136

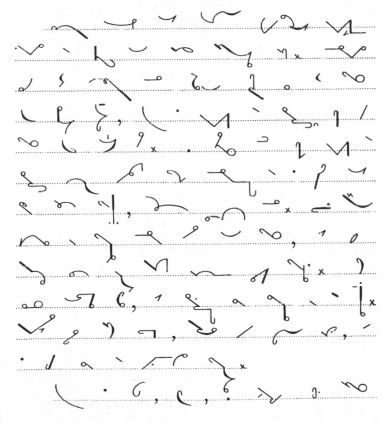

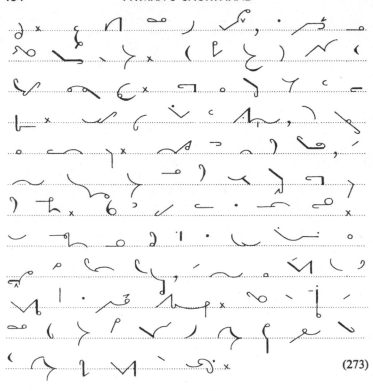

(273)

Exercise 137

(*Write in Shorthand*)

1. William J. Anderson, *who-is* a professor at Acadia *University, has* recently compiled *a* book *of* quotations *from* Shakespeare. *An* examination *of-the* book shows *that-we-do*-not-*have* to-go *to-the* theatre *to*-hear-*the language of* Shakespeare, *for-we* use *his* terms *and*-phrases constantly *in-our* everyday speech. (53)

2. *We-are* so *familiar with-the*-many conveniences *which* science *has put within our* reach *that-we-do*-not realize or appreciate *the* debt *we owe to* science. Constant use *and familiarity with-the* various time-saving *and* labour-saving devices tend *to*-make-us *over*look *their* tremendous value. *The* contributions *to-our* comfort *and* convenience by men *of* scientific training *are* continuous, *and*-they-*have* made-*the* modern world *a wonderful* place *to*-live in. (76)

3. *The* treasurer prepares *a* statement *of-the financial* condition *of-the* company annually. *In-the* case *of a public* corporation, *this* statement *is usually sent to-the* stockholders. *A* comparison *with* previous annual reports, or *balance* sheets, shows *whether-the year's trad*ing *has-been more* or less profitable.   (48)

4. *It-is-the practice of large insurance* firms *to* invest *the* bulk *of-their* funds *in first mortgages on buildings*, homes, *and* farms. *It-is* considered *that* real estate *is* less liable *to* sudden changes *in* value, *and, therefore, there-is* less *danger of-the* companies' *having to* suffer *any financial* loss through *a* sudden drop *in-the* value *of-their* holdings.   (62)

5. *Dear-*Sir, Will-*you* please consider my application *for-the* position *of-*treasurer *in-your organization. I-believe-that I-have-the* necessary qualifications *and* experience, *and-I-*enclose *a* summary *of-them for-your information.* If-*it-is* convenient, *I-shall* appreciate *an opportunity to* discuss my application *with-you, and any* questions *you-*may desire *to* ask *can-be* answered fully *during-the* course *of-our* interview. *Yours-respect*fully,   (71)

CHAPTER XVIII

84. Figures

Figures *one* to *seven* and the figure *nine* are best represented by shorthand outlines when they stand alone. Other numbers, except round numbers, are represented by the ordinary arabic numerals. Round numbers are represented as follows—

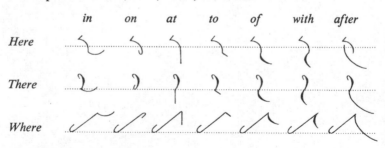

for *hundred* or *hundredth*; 7 700, 2 £200

for *thousand*; 5 5,000, 2 £2,000, 3 300,000

for *million*; 4 4,000,000, 2 200,000,000

for *billion*; 2 two billions

for *dollar*; 2 two billion dollars

85. Compound Words

Compounds of *here*, *there*, *where*, are written as follows—

	in	on	at	to	of	with	after
Here							
There							
Where							

86. Intersections

The practice of intersecting one stroke through another is a very useful device for the representation of very commonly occurring phrases.

The device may be adapted to meet the special needs of the writer. Thus, for some shorthand writers the stroke *p* might usefully represent the word *party*, whereas in an insurance office the stroke *p* might better be used to represent *policy*.

Where intersection is not practicable, write one stroke close to another.
The following list shows how the device may be used—

P represents *party*   Conservative Party

B   „   *bank* or *bill*   bank rate

                              city bank

                              bill of lading

T   „   *attention*   early attention

D   „   *department*   foreign department

CH   „   *charge*   this charge

                              free of charge

J   „   *Journal*   Bankers' Journal

                              Journal of Commerce

K   „   *company,*   this company
          cover, or
          captain   under separate cover

                              Captain Thompson

G   „   *government*   government official

G (with *n* hook)
    represents *beginning*   at the beginning

F represents *form*   necessary form

                              as a matter of form

TH	represents	*month*		in a month's time
				for a month
				next month
S	,,	*society*		agricultural society
M	,,	*manager,* *morning,* or *mark*		general manager
				Monday morning
				auditor's mark
N	,,	*national*		national affairs
L	,,	*limited*		Robinson, Limited
RAY	,,	*require-d-ment,* or *railway*		you may require
				will be required
				your requirements
				railway officials
R	,,	*arrange-d-ment*		please make arrangements
				we have arranged
Kr	,,	*corporation,* or *colonel*		public corporation
				Colonel Alexander
Pr	,,	*professor*		Professor Jackson

SHORT FORMS

inconvenience-t-ly, *distinguish-ed*, *income*, *become*, *becoming*, *welcome*, *nevertheless*.

Exercise 138

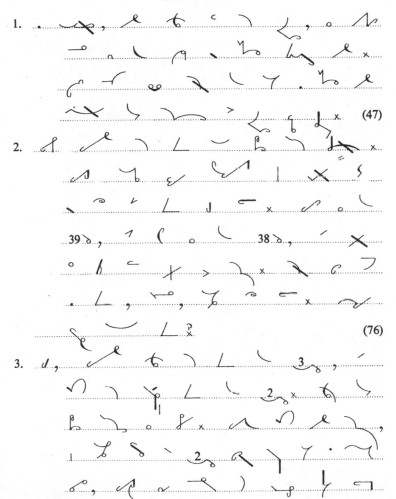

1. (47)

2. (76)

3.

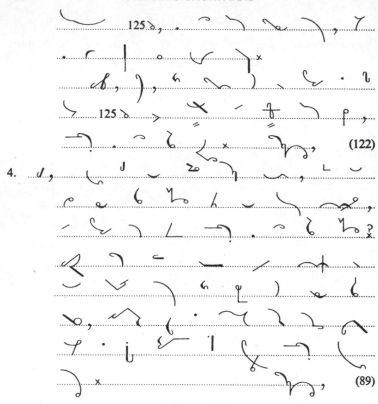

(122)

4.

(89)

Exercise 139

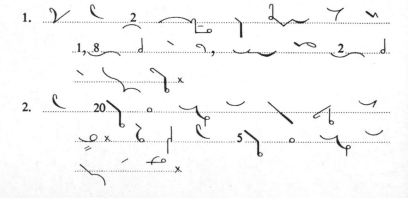

1.

2.

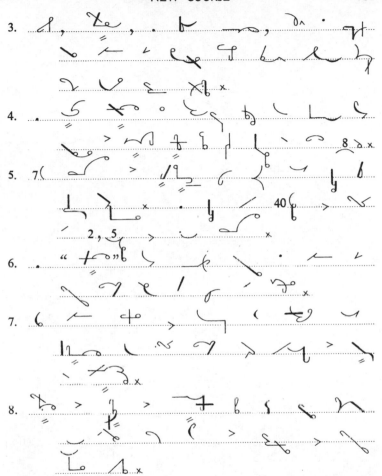

Exercise 140

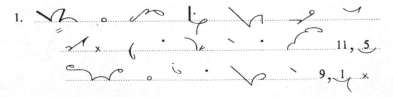

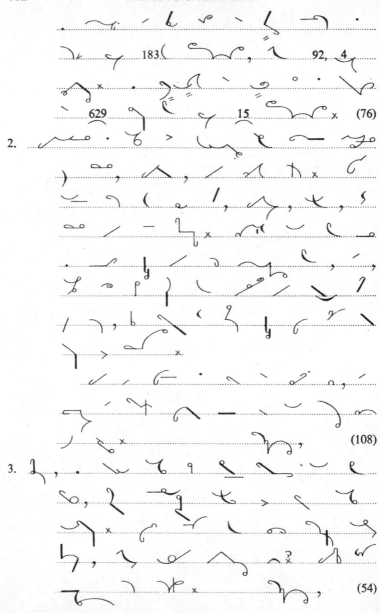

183(, 92, 4

629 15 x (76)

2.

x

x

(108)

3.

x

(54)

Short Forms

LIST ONE

The number in parenthesis indicates the chapter in which the word is presented.

A

a (4)

accord-ing (14)

acknowledge (15)

advantage (12)

advertise-
-ment-d (16)

all (9)

altogether (10)

an (4)

and (6)

any (5)

anything (9)

are (6)

as (8)

as is (9)

B

balance (12)

balanced (12)

be (1)

because (8)

become (18)

becoming (18)

been (12)

behalf (12)

belief (11)

believe-d (11)

beyond (7)

build-ing (11)

but (1)

C

call (11)

called (11)

can (5)

cannot (12)

care (11)

cared (14)

certificate (15)

chair (11)

chaired (14)

character (15)

cheer (11)

cheered (14)

child (14)

circumstance (16)

cold (11)

come (3)

commercial-
-ly (16)

could (10)

D

danger (17)

dear (11)

deliver-y-ed (11)

description (11)

different-ce (5)

difficult (12)

difficulty (12)

distinguish-
-ed (18)

do (1)

doctor, Dr. (11)

during (11)

E

English (17)

equal-ly (11)

equalled (11)

especial-ly (9)

everything (11)

exchange-d (17)

expect-ed (10)

eye (7)

F

familiar-ity (17)

February (10)

financial-ly (17)

first (9)

for (4)

from (11)

G

general-ly (12)

gentleman (12)

gentlemen (12)

give-n (3)

go (5)

gold (12)

govern-ed (16)

government (16)

great (12)

guard (12)

H

had (4)

hand (15)

has (8)

have (2)

he (7)

him (3)

himself (9)

his (8)

hour (6)

how (7)

however (11)

I

I (7)

immediate (15)

important--ce (14)

impossible (14)

improve-d--ment (14)

in (5)

income (18)

inconvenience--t-ly (18)

individual-ly (16)

influence (9)

influenced (9)

inform-ed (10)

information (13)

inscribe-d (16)

inscription (16)

inspect-ed--ion (10)

instruction (16)

instructive (16)

insurance (10)

interest (15)

investigation (13)

is (8)

is as (9)

it (1)

itself (9)

J

January (10)

K

knowledge (15)

L

language (9)

large (6)

largely (11)

larger (11)

largest (9)

liberty (11)

Lord (3)

M

me (7)

member (11)

mere (11)

more (11)

mortgage-d (17)

most (9)

Mr. (11)

much (9)

myself (9)

N

near (11)

neglect-ed (17)

never (10)

nevertheless (18)

New York (9)

next (9)

nor (11)

northern (12)

nothing (9)

November (10)

number-ed (11)

O

object-ed (13)

objection (13)

of (4)

on (4)

opinion (12)

opportunity (14)

organization (13)

organize-d (13)

ought (5)

our (6)

ourselves (9)

over (11)

owe (5)

owing (9)

own (11)

owner (11)

P

particular (14)

people (11)

pleasure (11)

practic(s)e-d (17)

principal-ly (11)

principle (11)

probable-
-ly-ility (16)

prospect (16)

public (13)

publication (13)

publish-ed (13)

put (5)

Q

quite (10)

R

rather (15)

regular (16)

remarkable (11)

remark-ed (11)

remember-
-ed (11)

represent-
-ed (12)

representative
(12)

respect-ed (10)

respectful-
-ly (11)

responsible-
-ility (12)

S

satisfaction (13)

satisfactory (10)

school (15)

schooled (15)

sent (10)

several (8)

shall (2)

short (15)

should (6)

significance (16)

significant (16)		third (12)	
signify-ied (16)		this (8)	
something (9)		those (8)	
southern (12)		though (9)	
speak (8)		thus (8)	
special-ly (8)		till (11)	
spirit (15)		to (1)	
subject-ed (8)		to be (5)	
sufficient--ly-cy (16)		together (10)	
sure (11)		told (12)	
surprise (11)		too (1)	
surprised (11)		toward (12)	
		trade (12)	

T

telegram (17)		tried (12)	
tell (11)		truth (11)	
thank-ed (6)		two (1)	
that (10)			

U

the (1)	under (15)	
their (11)	United States (9)	
them (2)	university (17)	
themselves (9)	usual-ly (2)	

V

there (11)	very (11)

W

therefore (15)		
thing (3)	was (2)	
think (2)	we (3)	

welcome (18)	
what (7)	
whatever (16)	
when (7)	
whenever (16)	
whether (14)	
which (1)	
who (1)	
whose (6)	
why (7)	
wish (5)	
wished (10)	
with (7)	
within (12)	
without (10)	
wonderful-ly (15)	
word (15)	
would (7)	
writer (15)	

Y

yard (15)	
year (6)	
you (7)	
young (9)	
your (6)	
yesterday (13)	

Short Forms

LIST TWO

The Short Forms given in the text are for words that are very frequently used. The following additional short forms will be found useful in high-speed writing. The words occur in lists of the ten thousand commonest words.

A

administrator

appointment

arbitrary

arbitration

architect-ure-al

assignment

B

bankruptcy

C

capable

characteristic

contentment

D

dangerous

defective ·

deficient-ly-cy

demonstrate

demonstration

destruction

discharge-d

E

efficient-ly-cy

electric

electrical

electricity

emergency

England

enlarge

enlargement

entertainment

enthusiastic-m

establish-ed-ment

executive

executor

expediency

expenditure

expensive

I

identical

identification

imperfect-ion-ly

incorporated

independent-ly-ce

indispensable-ly

influential-ly

intelligence

intelligent-ly

introduction

investment

irregular

J

jurisdiction

justification

L

legislative

legislature

M

manufacture-d

manufacturer

manuscript

mathematics

maximum

mechanical-ly

messenger

minimum

ministry

misfortune

monstrous

N

negligence

notwithstanding

O

objectionable

objective

P

passenger

peculiar-ity

perform-ed

performance

practicable

prejudice-d-ial-ly

preliminary

production

productive

project-ed

proportion-ed

prospective		stranger	
publisher		subscribe-d	
		subscription	
Q		substantial-ly	
questionable-ly		suspect-ed	
		sympathetic	
R		**T**	
reform-ed			
remarkable		telegraphic	
representation		thankful	
republic		**U**	
republican		unanimous-ly	
respective		uniform-ity-ly	
respectively		universal	
		universe	
S		**V**	
selfish-ness			
sensible-ly-ility		valuation	

Short Forms

LIST THREE

The following Short Forms do not occur in lists of the ten thousand commonest words.

A

abandonment

administratrix

amalgamate

amalgamation

arbitrate

arbitrator

attainment

C

circumstantial

contingency

cross-examination

cross-examine-d

D

denomination-al

destructive

destructively

E

enlarger

enlightenment

executrix

exigency

extinguish-ed

F

falsification

familiarization

familiarize

G

generalization

H

henceforward

howsoever

I

imperturbable

inconsiderate

informer

intelligible-ly

irrecoverable-ly

irremovable-ly

irrespective

irrespectively

irresponsible-ility

M

magnetic-ism

mathematical-ly

mathematician

metropolitan

O

obstruction

obstructive

oneself

organizer

P

performer

perpendicular

perspective

proficient-ly-cy

proportionate-ly

prospectus

R

recoverable

reformer

relinquish-ed

remonstrance

remonstrate

removable

reproduction

retrospect

retrospection

retrospective

S

signification

stringency

subjection

subjective

T

thenceforward

U

unanimity

universality

unprincipled

W

whensoever

whereinsoever

wheresoever

whithersoever

INDEX

*References are to the **paragraph** numbers unless otherwise stated*

GUIDE TO HIGH SPEED WRITING IN PITMAN'S SHORTHAND.
By EMILY D. SMITH, F.S.C.T., *Holder of National Union of Teachers Certificate for 250 words a minute*; and A. J. MUNRO. Gives sound instruction and practical advice dealing with every aspect of the training of the shorthand writer. **6s. 6d.**

MODEL SHORTHAND SPEED TESTS. 80–140 words a minute.
With an Introduction in shorthand by A. J. MUNRO. Each section contains twenty-three passages covering a wide variety of subjects and these will be found invaluable in preparing students for shorthand speed examinations. **6s.**

FOUR MINUTE SPEED TESTS.
Designed to meet the requirements of the Royal Society of Arts Shorthand Speed Examinations, etc. The speeds range from 80 to 140 words a minute. **3s. 6d.**

FIVE MINUTE SPEED TESTS.
This book contains eighty passages, counted in quarter-minutes, at speeds from 80 words a minute to 160 words a minute. **5s.**

TESTS FOR SPEED STUDENTS.
A series of interesting articles on widely varied subjects, the first section being in shorthand, and the second, which forms the Key, in letterpress. **6s.**

MISCELLANEOUS DICTATION TESTS FOR SHORTHAND STUDENTS.
This book contains a wide selection of articles on varied subjects, suitable for dictation to advanced speed classes. **6s. 6d.**

700 COMMON-WORD READING AND DICTATION EXERCISES.
A list of 700 recurring words and their derivatives, specially selected for the teaching of Pitman's Shorthand in English, together with reading and dictation exercises using only the words listed. In two books. **4s.** each.

PITMAN

PITMAN'S
SHORTHAND READING BOOKS
A SELECTION

Elementary Stage

Reading Lessons, No. 1 . . . . . 1s. 9d.
  Key. 1s. 9d.

Short Stories.   Vol. I . . . . . . 2s.
                    Vol. II . . . . . 1s. 9d.

Intermediate Stage

Alice's Adventures in Wonderland
  By LEWIS CARROLL . . . . 6s.

Reading Lessons, No. 2 . . . . . 1s. 9d.
  Key. 1s. 9d.

Advanced Stage

Thoughts and Theories
  By I. J. PITMAN, M.A. . . . . . . 3s. 6d.

Treasure Island
  By ROBERT LOUIS STEVENSON . . . . . 8s.

Hansel and Grethel
  By GRIMM . . . . 2s.

Reading Lessons, No. 3 . . . . . 2s. 6d.
  Key. 2s. 6d.

Half-Hours With Popular Authors
  Compiled by A. JEFFREY MUNRO.
  Vol. I, 3s. 9d. Vol. II, 3s. 6d. Vol. IV, 3s.

Readings from Popular Authors
  Compiled by A. JEFFREY MUNRO . . . . 10s. 6d.

Selected Extracts from Favourite Authors
  Compiled by A. JEFFREY MUNRO . . . . 7s. 6d.

The Silent Judge, and Other Stories
  By MAXWELL CROOKS . . . . . . 2s. 3d.

The Return of Sherlock Holmes
  By SIR A. CONAN DOYLE.
  Vol. I, 6s. Vol. II, 7s. 6d. Vol. III, 7s. 6d.

PITMAN